LettsGuide

KW-764-001

Paris

Frederick Tingey

Charles Letts & Co Ltd
London, Edinburgh, München & New York

*To Anita,
who made Paris
come to life*

First published 1976
by Charles Letts and Company Limited
Diary House, Borough Road, London SE1 1DW
Second revised edition 1980

Designer: Ben Sands
Cover and illustrations: Ed Perera
Photograph: J Allan Cash Limited
Maps: Ray Martin

© Text: Frederick Tingey
ISBN 0 85097 470 4
Printed in Great Britain by
Charles Letts (Scotland) Ltd

Contents

The Eiffel Tower – symbol of Paris

1. Introduction

Cosomopolitan and stimulating, with a strong personality, Paris is one of the most fascinating cities in the world. It is also one of the most dignified and elegant, with incomparable vistas leading the eye to superb architectural features, as well as being a great storehouse of art of all periods. And few places have such abundant evidence of a long and varied history, much of it linked closely with our own.

In his account of the conquest of Gaul in 53BC Julius Caesar mentions the Parisii tribe living in a settlement called Lutetia on an island in the Seine, the present-day Ile de la Cité. The colony the Romans established there quickly extended to the left bank of the river, where traces of its buildings still exist. But it was still a colony, the centre of Roman Gaul being Lyon to the south. Introduced in the 3rd century by St Denis, the evangelist martyred on the hill of Montmartre, the Christian faith soon gained converts among both the local people and the Roman colonists. As Roman power declined in the late 4th century Lutetia gradually came to be known as Paris. According to legend, when Attila and his Huns stormed into Gaul the city was saved from destruction in 451 by the bravery of Geneviève, a pious virgin revered after her death as the patron saint of Paris.

Clovis, the first Frankish king baptised in 496 as a Christian, chose Paris for his capital. But the empire he built up was fragmented by the Merovingian kings and their heirs who succeeded him and, in the 8th century, by the invading Saracens fighting under the banner of Islam – until turned back by Charles Martel, an able military leader who assumed power. In 751 his son Pepin the Short sent the last Merovingian monarch to a monastery and was himself elected king of the Franks, the Pope annointing him in 754 at the abbey church of St Denis. Merovingian rule was based on a rural economy in which towns played little part, and Paris remained much as it had been under the Romans, a small provincial town. It was little different after Pepin's son Charles, known as Charlemagne (from

Carolus Magnus, or Charles the Great), was made ruler in 768 of the vast kingdom created by his father.

Within a generation of the death of Charlemagne in 814 the empire was a shambles, the murderous Vikings sailing their longboats up the Seine without hindrance in 845 to sack and burn Paris, vulnerable like all other towns in Gaul. Yet even from this turbulent period some buildings have survived, among them the basilica housing the shrine of St Denis on the northern outskirts, the tower of St Germain des Près and the little church of St Julien le Pauvre. In 987 the last enfeebled Carolingian king died and the nobles elected Hugues Capet as king. Under the Capets the fortifications of Paris were extended and within the walls several monasteries sprang up. The Capets controlled little territory but they did confirm Paris as their capital, and from this time on it was around Paris that the French nation took shape. Evidence of these times still exists in the Louvre and Notre Dame.

During the reign of Phillippe Auguste (1189-1223) Paris was transformed into one of the most important cities in Europe. By the beginning of the 13th century there were over 20,000 foreign students attending the university. This king, companion in arms of Richard the Lionheart, was the first to pave the principal streets with stone and establish a central market, but it was his successor Louis IX (a name derived from Clovis) who beautified Paris with some of the most impressive Gothic architecture ever built, the Sainte Chapelle and the west front of Notre Dame cathedral. Known as Saint Louis because of his piety, Louis IX also reorganized the university (recognized by the Pope in 1215) and encouraged the founding of schools and colleges. One, established by his chaplain Robert de Sorbon in 1252, was to become the centre around which university life in Paris revolved. Paris was not only the capital of France, it was also the capital of learning of the Western world, French having become the *lingua franca* even of the English court. Then, as now, all distances to other parts of France were measured from the parvis or open space fronting the portal of Notre Dame.

Life was more unsettled in the years that followed, with

The façade of Notre Dame Cathedral

rivalry between the feudal barons and many uprisings in the city, most of them because the Parisians wanted more say in their own affairs, particularly in the levying of taxes. A reminder of these years are the towers of the Conciergerie, the headquarters of officials charged with punishing speculators in food.

Charles IV, the last direct descendant of St Louis, having left no heir, the monarchy passed to the house of Valois. Edward III of England, nephew of the last of the Capets, laid claim to the throne of France. The result was the Hundred Years' War. Two of the biggest setbacks for the French were their crushing defeat at the battles of Crécy and Poitiers. In the second battle the French king Jean II was made prisoner of the Black Prince and held hostage in England, while the Parisians were exploited by the rival factions of the Burgundians and Armagnacs, who frequently fought in the streets.

In 1421 Paris was occupied by the English, who were not forced out until 1446 during the reign of Charles VII. His heir Louis XI eventually bought off the English king and emphasized the civic importance of Paris so as to weaken the power of the nobles. The late Gothic architecture built during this time includes the churches of St Séverin, St Eustache and the Hôtel de Sens.

Paris was enriched in the years that followed by the links established with Italy as a result of the campaigns of Charles VIII, Louis XII, and François I, which had a profound effect on art in the capital as it did in the rest of Europe. Italian artists worked in the city while French architects studied in Rome. On their return to France they introduced a new spirit into architecture, converting the medieval fortress of the Louvre into a splendid palace for François I, building monumental bridges across the Seine, and decorating the squares with beautiful fountains. These were prosperous times and the population of Paris increased to make it the biggest city in Western Europe.

But the new impetus to building was interrupted by the death during a jousting match of François' successor Henri II. For a while France was without a king. The vacuum was filled by the religious wars, and Paris, then a

Catholic stronghold, only recognized Henri IV as king after he had announced his conversion to the faith. The first of the Bourbons, Henri IV extended the Louvre and built the Pont Neuf, the oldest surviving bridge in Paris, along with the elegant Place des Vosges. Over the next 200 years, during the reigns of four successive Louis' (Louis XIII, XIV, XV, and XVI), the dynasty rose to heights of grandeur then tailed off into impotence. The able minister of Louis XIII, the visionary Cardinal Richelieu, reconstructed the kingdom, founded the French Academy, rebuilt and extended the privileges of the Sorbonne and encouraged the French theatre.

As Paris continued to grow so it established itself as the centre of the arts, an irresistible magnet for writers and artists from all over France. While Louis XIV was still a child Mazarin became even more powerful a figure than Richelieu had been, but when Mazarin died Louis XIV took over the reins himself. In 1682, happy to quit Paris and the Louvre, he made Versailles his principal residence. His scrupulous minister Colbert was active in almost every sphere yet still found time to set up the Academy of Science in 1666 and the Academy of Architecture in 1671. He regulated Richelieu's French Academy, and reorganized the Academy of Painting and Sculpture, also established by Richelieu. In 1663 he put Le Brun in charge of the Gobelins manufactory, a royal institution committed to supplying tapestries and other furnishings for Louis XIV's many palaces.

Cultural life in Paris sparkled with the plays of Molière, Racine and Corneille, the stirring sermons of Bossuet, the animal fables of La Fontaine, the new philosophy of Descartes, and the dissertations on religion and morals of Pascal. In 1683 Colbert died and was succeeded by Louvois, who struggled to finance Louis XIV's foreign wars as Colbert had struggled for 20 years to pay for the luxury imposed by the Grand Monarch. At least government was centralized and national unity was an established fact.

During Louis XIV's reign more than a hundred new streets were added to the capital's network, lit at night by over 6,500 lanterns. At great expense Louvois developed the octagonal Place Vendôme and the Pont Royal bridge. A whole new quarter of great houses sprang up round the Palais du Luxembourg on the Left Bank. Paris remains studded with monuments to the Sun King, among them the Place des Victoires, the Hôtel Carnavalet, and the vast Hôtel des Invalides, built to house soldiers wounded in his service.

Louis died in 1715 but his wars, extravagance, and conceit had bankrupted France, and his autocratic rule and oppressive taxes had fostered great discontent among the people.

The boy king Louis XV, the regent, and their many advisers only made matters worse. Yet French commerce expanded and strong links were established with the New World. A series of wars, at the end of which France gave up all claims to Canada, depleted the country even further. In 1748 Montesquieu condemned the monarchy in France and encouraged a flowering of rational inquiry which brought into the open all the controversies that previously had been forced underground. Louis XV died unlamented in 1747. Barely 20 when he came to the throne, Louis XVI was even more incapable than his predecessor. In fact, by siding with the colonists against the British in the American War of Independence he helped bring about his own downfall. Frenchmen had seen how freedom could be won, and did not forget it.

On July 14, twelve years after the tide of war in America had turned in favour of the colonists, the Paris mob stormed the great royal fortress and prison of the Bastille. This set in motion a train of violent events, with political rivalries leading to more excesses as one class grew to hate and fear the other. In 1793 the king, the queen, and many of their courtiers went to the guillotine in a riot of hysteria and bloodshed astonishing in a people priding itself on its logic and rational behaviour. At least the Revolution of 1789-99 did change some things for the better.

But another tyrant was waiting in the wings. Trading on his popularity among the Revolutionaries and his military prowess, Napoleon Bonaparte seized power and soon set himself up as Emperor. While in office he reorganized the legal system, the roads, and much else, and put up many imposing monuments, but he brought about much more bloodshed before his final collapse in 1815.

Then France had two other kings who, though less reactionary than Louis XVI, were universally hated by the Parisians. In 1848 a more radical upheaval took place and Louis Napoleon, nephew of Napoleon I, became President and in 1852 Emperor. He appointed Haussmann Prefect of the Seine and began building the Paris of today.

Whole districts of crowded narrow streets were replaced by broad avenues and magnificent buildings erected regardless of cost. Haussmann first created the north-south boulevards to ease traffic congestion, the most important of which were the Boulevards St Michel, Palais, and Sébastopol. He then tackled the central area, laying out the Avenue de l'Opéra, the Boulevards Haussmann and Magenta, the Rue de Rivoli, and others. He extended the Champs Elysées, completed the Louvre and built the central market of Les Halles. Enormous sums were tied up in this work.

When France surrendered to Germany in 1870 the Second Empire established by Napoleon III collapsed and a republic was proclaimed. The Prussians laid seige to Paris in September 1870 and in the following January the city signed a treaty of surrender with Bismarck. While the government was negotiating with the Germans the Paris Commune took over the city: over 30,000 people were killed and many public buildings destroyed before the uprising was put down. At the turn of the century Paris played a big part in the reconstruction of France. Great world exhibitions were staged in the capital in 1878, 1889 (celebrating the centenary of the Revolution), and 1900, focussing foreign interest on the city as never before and establishing it as a cultural centre of the first rank.

Paris was bombed from the air during the 1914-18 war but little damage was done, though in spring 1918 shells fired from the German long-range gun Big Bertha killed 88 people in the church of St Gervais-St-Protais.

The city became a world tourist centre during the Twenties and Thirties, two million people visiting it each year.

When the Germans invaded France in June 1940 the capital was declared an open city and those Parisians who had not hastily grabbed what possessions they could carry and headed south stayed in their homes as the troops of the Wehrmacht goose-stepped down the Champs Elysées. The Kommandatur of Greater Paris made the Hôtel Meurice in the Rue de Rivoli his headquarters, while the Luftwaffe occupied the Palais du Luxembourg. The road signs that soon appeared at the Place de l'Opéra were all in German, which created no problems since the only vehicles on the streets were those driven by the Gestapo or the military. Even the pavements in front of buildings requisitioned by the Germans were put out of bounds to Parisians.

Within a year or two many of the citizens were starving. At the Tuileries, the gardeners uprooted the flowers and planted tomatoes. The daily ration of bread varied between 8 oz and 1 lb according to one's age and type of work. The meat ration fell to 1 lb a month. But anyone with enough money could buy everything he needed on the black market.

The Germans mobilized the small factories in the city, ordering them to turn out tanks, torpedoes, and aircraft parts. When night fell, most Parisians tuned in secretly to the BBC. Others organized themselves into resistance groups: many were arrested, tortured, deported or executed.

As Allied troops drew near the capital under the blazing sun of August 1944 Hitler ordered General von Choldiz, the commander of Greater Paris, to evacuate the city only after destroying as much of it as possible, notably blowing up 62 bridges across the Seine. But Choldiz was fortunately human and left quietly with most of his troops, leaving only a rearguard. Resistance fighters took over the Hôtel de Ville and other buildings but it soon became clear that Paris could only be liberated from outside. Once the French Leclerc division had routed the remaining German troops the way was clear for Général de Gaulle to make his triumphant walk down the Champs Elysées among the enthusiastic crowds.

As part of the regeneration of France that followed the rebuilding, the population of Paris continued to grow, many of the immigrants being French settlers forced out of former colonies and called *pieds noirs* or black feet by the natives of those countries unused to the sight of people wearing shoes. During the eleven years of his tenure de Gaulle appointed André Malraux minister of cultural affairs and under his direction the monuments of Paris were cleaned of their sooty film, and historical districts like the Marais were restored to something like their former glory. The Sorbonne, the main centre of higher education in France, became in May 1968 the focal point of student unrest that initiated reforms in the university system all over France.

Paris is now ringed by high-rise suburbs and satellite towns and even within the city itself there are new developments in being or planned. Yet along with its historic monuments, it has preserved its essential character in a way few other cities have paralleled.

2. Getting Around

Getting there

The cheapest way to get to Paris from London is by
hovercraft and coach (Hoverlloyd) or train (Seaspeed).
Overnight travel by rail and ferry costs only a little more,
whereas day travel is expensive. Other combinations are
coach-air via Lydd and Beauvais (Dan Air), and rail-air
via Gatwick and le Touquet (British Caledonian). The
quickest way to travel between London and Paris but
costing at least one third as much again is by scheduled
air service (Air France and British Airways). Youth (under
18) and student return fares are available on the hovercraft-
coach/train and coach-air routes. Senior citizens may also
travel at reduced rates.

The shortest cross-Channel car ferry routes for Paris, about
100 minutes, are from Folkestone and Dover to Boulogne
and Calais. This is also the longest road route, Paris being
about 180 miles from either French port. A longer crossing
(around 4 hours) from Newhaven lands motorists at
Dieppe, only 100 miles from Paris. From Rouen, south of
Dieppe, the fast A13 motorway (toll) joins the express ring
road encircling Paris at the Porte de St Cloud. The main
road from Calais and Boulogne (the N1) joins the ring road
at the massive interchange of Porte de la Chapelle.

When to go

Spring and autumn are the best times to visit Paris, not
between July and September when the city is barely
ticking over and least of all in August when many
restaurants, shops, and theatres are closed for their
fermeture annuelle. The Paris 'season' runs from early
May to mid-July. This is when the city looks its best: the
parks and gardens are at their most attractive, the shop
displays at their most inviting, the main buildings are
floodlit, and many exhibitions and shows are put on.

Orientation

While it may not cover as large an area as London, Paris
is the most densely populated city in Europe and

confusing enough for the first-time visitor. It is useful to remember that the Sacré Coeur church is on the north, the Eiffel Tower on the southwest, and the Maine-Montparnasse tower on the south. The Seine flows into the city on the east, and divides to pass the two islands of the Cité and St Louis, the two arms joining up to separate the Right and Left Bank before swinging southwest to pass the Eiffel Tower. The two banks are connected by no fewer than 26 bridges.

The largest part of Paris is on the Right Bank, where most of the historic monuments, the great boulevards and museums are. Inside the Grands Boulevards many of the streets are called *rues*. The French for suburb is *faubourg* and those streets crossing the boulevards became *rue du faubourg*. After crossing the Boulevard Montmartre the Rue Montmartre, for example, becomes the Rue du Faubourg Montmartre. The numbers of streets on a north-south line start at the end nearest the Seine, those running east-west on the east. Paris is divided into some 20 *arrondissements* corresponding to the London boroughs. There are nearly 800 miles of streets in Paris and the names of some of them are frequently changed. This is the result of the French authorities tending to name their streets after people they consider important at the time.

Autobus and Métro

The easiest and quickest way to travel in Paris is by métro. Created in 1900, the Chemin de Fer Métropolitain (16 lines, 350 stations) operates from 05.30 to 01.15. Each line takes the names of the places where it begins and ends. There are two classes, first and second, and the fare is the same no matter how far you travel or how many times you change. (Inter-changes are called *correspondances*). Special seats are reserved for pregnant women, war veterans, and old people.

Time-keeping of the buses operated by the state-run RATP (Régie Autonome des Transports Parisiens) has been improved by reserving special lanes for them, as in London, though services are still slow during rush hours. The buses operate on numbered lines divided into sections from 06.30 or 07.20 to 20.30 or 21.00. Fares are one-class and you pay according to the number of sections over which you travel (rarely more than two in the central area). There are timetables at main bus stops. All-night services operate from the Place du Châtelet (Avenue Victoria) to the outskirts every hour between 01.00 and 06.00. Services of all buses are considerably reduced on Sundays and public holidays. Yet the *autobus* provides the cheapest sightseeing in Paris.

Save money with a *carnet* of 10 tickets (valid on bus and métro) or a four or seven-day *billet de tourisme* with which you can travel as often and as far as you like. The *carnet* can be bought at métro stations, *tabacs,* and shops displaying the RATP sign, the *billet* can be obtained (on presentation of passport) at the Services Touristiques de la RATP, 53 bis Quai des Grands Augustins [7B3], 20 Place de la Madeleine [3E1], and at main railway and métro stations. The RATP organizes over 70 excursions within and beyond Paris at a moderate price, some with guide-interpreter. The tours start near the Marché aux Fleurs in the Place de la Madeleine.

Taxis Paris has plenty of taxis – until you want one. Fares (based on the time of day and distance travelled) are high. Radio taxis can be called on 587.67.89, 735.22.22, 205.77.00 and 267.28.30.

Motoring

Except perhaps in the rush hour, motorists can drive round Paris in three quarters of an hour on the *boulevards périphériques* encircling the capital on the line of the historic old *portes* or gates; these express ring roads are dual carriageway and without traffic lights or crossroads. There are turn-offs at each *porte* and the important thing to remember is to mentally tick off those preceding the one you want and to get into the filter lane in good time to catch it. Cars towing caravans or trailers are banned from many streets within the area bounded by the *boulevards périphériques*.

If you are spending only a day or two in Paris you might prefer to leave your car at a *parking* near one of the *portes* on the *boulevards périphériques* and go on from there by bus or métro. This is feasible if you are not carrying a lot of luggage, but for a longer stay your own car is still very useful in the evenings and at weekends.

Driving in Paris can be a stimulating experience once you know the rules. The French drive with spirit, and traffic moves much faster than it does in London.

Traffic on main roads in France usually has priority but in towns, cars – or anything else on wheels – emerging from junctions (including roundabouts) on the right take precedence, and it is just as well to be prepared for them. The answer is to ignore everything on your left and concentrate on giving way to traffic crossing your path from the right. The police impose on-the-spot fines for traffic offences like not ceding priority when necessary, as well as for parking in the wrong place (near bus stops, facing the traffic) or for too long. A new feature on the Paris traffic scene are the *aubergines* or women traffic wardens.

The only way to cope with the maze of one-way streets in the capital is to have a map of them and refer to it frequently. Paris is notorious for its traffic congestion, caused mainly by most Parisians living in apartment buildings and having to leave their cars in the street. Finding somewhere to park by the kerb can be a long and frustrating business, and a better bet is to use one of the underground car parks.

There are underground car parks or *parkings souterrains* beneath the Avenue Foch (Etoile), Rond Point des Champs Elysées, Concorde, Place de la Madeleine, the Galeries Lafayette (Boulevard Haussmann), Place Vendôme, Place du Marché St Honoré, Palais de Justice (Ile de la Cité), Parvis Notre Dame, Esplanade des Invalides, the Panthéon, Gare Montparnasse, Centre Beaubourg and many other places.

When motoring in Paris keep handy some one-franc coins in case you find a space at a parking meter. Even if there are no meters most of the central area is in the *zone bleue*, where you must display in your windscreen a parking disc obtainable from garages, *tabacs*, and newsagents showing what time you left the car. When you set the disc it indicates how long you may park: an hour or more depending on the time of day.

Walking
When crossing the street is pays to be specially careful for the first day or two, remembering to look left not right when stepping off the kerb. There are controlled crossings (marked by a double row of metal studs) at main junctions, but elsewhere the only way to get across is to wait for a gap in the traffic, walk into the middle of the road, and wait for a break in the stream flowing in the opposite direction. The golden rule is either to go forward or stand still; never turn back, as Parisian drivers are taught to steer behind anyone crossing the street.

3. Champs Elysées, Etoile, Chaillot

The fashionable heart of 19th-century Paris, with its grand hotels, sophisticated shops, and luxurious private houses, is centred on the great Avenue des Champs Elysées, the world's most impressive thoroughfare.

At one end of it, the splendid Place de la Concorde [2F6], one of the best-known squares of any capital, is a vantage point for superb vistas: the Tuileries Gardens and the Champs Elysées on the east and west, the Madeleine and Palais Bourbon on the north and south.

A magnificent sight at night, the square is open on all sides except the north, where it is bordered by fine 18th century buildings designed by Gabriel, the architect of Versailles. Among them are the luxurious Hôtel Crillon and the Ministry of Marine, the French equivalent of our Admiralty. The entrance to the Tuileries Gardens on the east side of the square is dominated by the Chevaux de Marly, winged horses bearing the figures of Mercury and Fame, set up in 1795.

Islanded by the traffic, the obelisk in the centre of the square is a granite monolith 75 ft high, once part of the temple of Luxor built by Rameses II. It was given to the French king Louis Philippe by Mohammed Ali, ruler of Egypt, in 1836. The two great fountains on either side of the obelisk were built between 1836 and 1846 at the same time as the nearby pavilions, decorated with statues personifying the eight principal towns of France: Lyon, Marseille, Bordeaux, Nantes, Rouen, Brest, Lille, and Strasbourg.

The Place de la Concorde is associated with one of the most turbulent periods in French history. The north side of the square remains as it was in Revolutionary days, when it was the usual place of execution. Over a two-year period, around 1,200 people were guillotined there. The first to die were the king and queen, Louis XVI and Marie Antoinette, followed by many of the nobility, members of moderate political parties, and finally Robespierre and other initiators of the Terror.

The lavishly decorated Petit Palais

From the west side of the square the wide Avenue des Champs Elysées sweeps majestically for over a mile up to the Arc de Triomphe. As far as the Rond Point [2E5] the avenue is flanked by the beautiful gardens of the Champs Elysées or Elysian Fields. Isolated in the gardens on the north side of the avenue are the Théâtre Marigny and several expensive restaurants. The gardens are bounded on the north by the Avenue Gabriel, overlooked by the rear of the British Embassy and the Elysée Palace, official residence of the president of the French Republic. Set in the gardens reaching down to the Seine on the south side of the Avenues des Champs Elysées are the ornately decorated Petit and Grand Palais [2F5], built, like the avenue between them and the adjoining Pont Alexandre III, for the 1900 exhibition. On the north side of the Petit Palais is a monument to Georges Clemenceau, Prime Minister of France during the last two years of the 1914-18 war. Officially known as the Palais des Beaux Arts, the Petit Palais houses paintings and sculpture owned by the municipality of Paris (see p 61). The main entrance is in the Avenue Winston Churchill.

The west part of the Grand Palais is named the Palais de la Découverte, a science museum created for the 1937 exhibition and entered from the Avenue Franklin Roosevelt: fascinating displays and demonstrations illustrate discoveries in biology, medicine, astronomy, mathematics, chemistry, physics and nuclear energy (see p 62).

Six avenues meet at the Rond Point [2E5], decorated with flower beds and fountains illuminated at night. Between the roundabout and the Arc de Triomphe the Avenue des Champs Elysées is lined with hotels, cafés, cinemas, banks, car showrooms, and the offices of airlines and multi-national companies. On the left is a wealthy residential district, the Quartier Marbeuf. On the right-hand side of the avenue, highlighted by the coaches, usually double-parked outside, is the famous *grand cabaret* of the Lido.

Twelve great avenues radiate like the spokes of a wheel from the vast circular Place Charles de Gaulle [1D3], still referred to by its former name of Etoile. In the centre is the huge Arc de Triomphe, the world's biggest triumphal arch, 160ft high and 148ft wide, planned by Napoleon to celebrate French military glory, and only completed in 1836 after his exile and death. Most remarkable of the many bas-reliefs that decorate it is the Départ, otherwise known as the Marseillaise, by the great French sculptor François Rude. The arch straddles the tomb of the Unknown Soldier of the 1914-18 war, lit at the foot by the Eternal Flame, focal point of patriotic demonstrations such as those held on Armistice Day. Inside is a small museum (closed Tuesdays) devoted to the history of the monument, reached by stairs or lift to the top, from which there is a remarkable view.

From the Etoile the elegant Avenue Foch, the widest street in Paris (nearly 400ft) and still one of the best addresses in the capital, leads to the extensive park of the Bois de Boulogne [1D1], about a mile away, with racecourses, lakes, gardens, and the beautiful château of Bagatelle.

Prolonging the Avenue des Champs Elysées west of the Etoile is the great Avenue de la Grande Armée, which runs ruler-straight to the ultra-modern developments of Porte Maillot and the skyscraper complex of La Défense dominated by the Tour Fiat, with its *bar-restaurant gastronomique* on the 44th floor. The Avenue Kléber runs in a straight line south from the Etoile to the Place du Trocadéro [1F2]. The Rue de Berry on the left leads to the Place des Etats Unis [1E3], with numerous American monuments: to the volunteers from the United States who fought on the side of the French in the 1914-18 war, to George Washington, to Lafayette and others.

At the southern end of the Avenue Kléber is the Place du Trocadéro [1F2], on the south side of which is the enormous Woolworth-style Palais de Chaillot built for the 1937 exhibition and once the meeting place of the League of Nations. It replaces the Trocadéro built for the 1878 exhibition and named after one of the forts at Cadiz in southern Spain taken by the French in 1823.

The two long wings of the building house four museums, with separate admission charges to each. In the north-east wing is the Musée des Monuments Français made up of casts of the works of the major French sculptors as well as copies of architectural features (see p 65) and the Musée Cinematheque with exhibits relating to the French cinema. The south-west wing houses the Musée de l'Homme, with extensive ethnographical collections (see p 63), and the Musée de la Marine, showing the history of the French navy and merchant shipping (see p 64).

From the terrace behind the Palais de Chaillot there are magnificent views of the gardens, the statue-decorated

Pont d'Iéna, the Eiffel Tower, and, beside the Seine on the south, the tower of the huge round ORTF radio centre.

West of the Trocadéro is the residential district of Passy, in an attractive location between the Bois de Boulogne and the Seine. In the noble Passy cemetery adjoining the Place du Trocadéro (but entered from the Avenue Paul Doumer) many distinguished people are buried, among them Debussy, Manet, and Gabriel Faure. The Avenue Paul Doumer runs south-west from the cemetery to its junction with the Rue de Passy [5A1]. Housed in a palatial mansion in the short Rue Louis Boilly, beyond the Ranelagh garden west of the junction, is the important Musée Marmottan [5A1], with a priceless art collection of various periods which includes a large number of paintings by Claude Monet (see p 65).

In the Rue Franklin leading south from the Place du Trocadéro is the house where the statesman Georges Clemenceau ('the Tiger') lived for 34 years until his death. It is now a museum (see p 62).

In the Rue Raynouard, which continues the Rue Franklin on the south, is one of the many houses lived in by that nomadic writer Honoré de Balzac [5B1], who never could make ends meet and moved frequently to avoid his creditors. In 1908 the municipality of Paris decided to make it a museum to house his few belongings (see p 61).

Spanning the Seine a short way south of the Rue Raynouard is the double-decked monumental Pont de Bir Hakeim [5A2], which straddles the eastern tip of a long narrow island called the Allée des Cygnes. On the Pont de Grenelle [5B1], at the far end of the island, is a replica of Bartholdi's famous Statue of Liberty at the entrance to New York harbour, presented by France in 1886. Americans living in Paris gave the replica to the city in 1889. The Avenue du Président Wilson leads east from the Place du Trocadéro to the Place d'Iéna [1F3], centred on a statue of George Washington paid for by donations from American women in memory of French help during the War of Independence. The Musée Guimet on the north side of the square contains one of the finest collections of Asiatic art in the world (see p 63).

East of the Place d'Iéna, the avenue du Président Wilson passes through the well-to-do district of Chaillot. On the left is the Musée d'Art Moderne de la Ville (see p 60) housed in a functional-style building put up for the 1937 exhibition. On the Seine side of the building is Bourdelle's statue of France, female figures of lesser artists, and the magnificent bas-reliefs of the muses by Alfred Janniot. The astonishing 19th-century renaissance-style palace in the Avenue Pierre ler de Serbie running north-east from the Place d'Iéna was given to the city of Paris by the Duchess of Galliera and now houses the Musée de la Mode et du Costume.

The Avenue du Président Wilson continues east to the Place de l'Alma [2F4], where seven roads meet. In the centre of the square is Bourdelle's impressive monument to the Polish poet Mickiewicz. Another monument nearby was erected by Belgium in 1923 in gratitude for French support during the 1914-18 war.

At the beginning of the Avenue Montaigne on the east side of the square is the beautiful façade of the huge Théâtre des Champs Elysées, built at the turn of the century, and in the Avenue George V is the American church, dating from 1888. On the piers of the Pont de l'Alma adjoining the square is the giant sculptured figure of the legendary Zouave or Moorish soldier; a time of danger is when the flood waters of the Seine reach up to his belt.

East along the right bank of the Seine the Cours Albert changes its name to Cours la Reine [2F5], named after its creator Marie de Médicis. It adjoins the sculpture-decorated single-span bridge of Pont Alexandre III, named in honour of the Russian Tsar, and daring in its conception for 1900. At its far end the Avenue Montaigne joins the Avenue des Champs Elysées at the Rond Point. Lining this street and the Rue François ler cutting across it are luxurious shops and the premises of the top couturiers: Dior, Balmain, and Courrèges.

4. Ile de la Cité, Ile St Louis

The Ile de la Cité and the Ile St Louis form the nucleus
of the original Paris, named after the Parisii tribe living
there when Julius Caesar conquered Gaul. Yet except for
the riverside quais that ring them round being equally
pleasant, the two islands are quite different in character.

The Ile de la Cité is like a ship anchored in the river, its
prow facing downstream, its moorings the eight bridges
joining it to the banks of the Seine on either side. Almost
wholly occupied by public buildings, it is still the centre of
civic life in Paris. The Ile St Louis, joined to the larger
island by a single bridge, is more peaceful and secretive
and essentially residential, with few monuments but some
fine houses.

Prolonging the Rue du Pont Neuf leading south from
Les Halles, the famous double-span Pont Neuf (despite
its name the oldest surviving bridge in Paris) leads to the
Place du Pont Neuf [7A3] at the western end of the Ile de
la Cité. West of the *place* is the Square du Vert Galant, a
popular name for Henri IV, commemorated by a statue.
Triangular rather than square, it is a vantage point for
views downstream and for boarding one of the *vedettes* or
pleasureboats of the Seine. Entered by a short street on the
east side of the Place du Pont Neuf is the classical Place
Dauphine, lined with three storey houses in brick and
stone, and occupied at street level by picture galleries and
antique shops.

Between the square and the busy Boulevard du Palais
crossing the island from north to south is the immense
Palais de Justice [7A3], the principal law courts of France,
integral with which are the Ste Chapelle, the Tour de
L'Horloge, and the Conciergerie. The building occupies
the site of a palace built in the early 14th century for the
Capetian kings, the only visible signs of which are the
square Tour de l'Horloge and three other towers on the
north side. Inside the building is the vast hall of the Salle
des Pas Perdus (Lost Steps), thronged with lawyers and
their clients when the courts are in session. This was the
great hall of the royal palace. Most of the courts are open

to visitors from 09.00 to 18.00 (except Sundays). Off the hall is the famous Chambre Dorée (Golden Room), once the royal bedroom, rich in 17th-century woodcarvings.

Consisting of two chapels, one above the other, the Sainte Chapelle is a marvel of Gothic architecture built in 1248 on the order of Louis IX (Saint Louis) to house the holy relics sent from Constantinople. The upper chapel, reserved for the royal family, is remarkable for the warm light that filters in from its beautiful stained glass windows made up of 1,100 separate panels, each illustrating a scene from the Bible.

Entered from the Quai de l'Horloge, on the north side of the building, [7a3], the Conciergerie takes its name from being the official residence of the Concierge or sheriff of the city. During the Revolution thousands of people were crammed into the prison to await execution, climbing the steps (now closed) near the main entrance to the law courts

The Conciergerie – former official residence of the Concierge

on their way to the tumbril and the guillotine. There are guided visits from 10.00 to 12.00 and from 13.00 to 17.00 (16.00 in winter). The building is closed on Tuesdays in summer and on Tuesdays and Fridays in winter.

Visitors can see the guard room, the impressive Salle de St Louis, and another hall decorated with four ornate fireplaces. Farther on is the Cour des Femmes – an exercise yard for women prisoners, the cells where Marie Antoinette and Robespierre spent their last hours, and a miniature museum made up of relics of the queen. The Conciergerie is still used as a prison for offenders on trial.

On the far side of the Boulevard du Palais is the Préfecture de Police or police headquarters [7B3]. Entered from the Rue des Carmes is the Musée de la Préfecture de Police containing an intimidating collection of uniforms, charge sheets and other documents, criminal weapons including home-made bombs, gas pistols, and a pair of sleeves maliciously studded with iron spikes (see p 66).

Where the nearby Rue de la Cité joins the Quai de la Corse [7B3] is the Marché aux Fleurs or flower market, joined on Sundays by a bird market. Occupying the southeast corner of the Ile de la Cité is the great cathedral of Notre Dame [8B4] built in 1163-1330, enlarged in the 17th century, and restored by Viollet-le-Duc in the 19th century. Set in the cobbles in the centre of the parvis fronting the cathedral is a copper hexagon, starting point of all main roads radiating from Paris.

Notable parts of the newly cleaned exterior of Notre Dame are the three splendid portals of the main façade and the flying buttresses and gargoyles of the apse. Inside, at the far end of the majestically proportioned nave lit by the great rose windows, is the impressive carved screen of the choir.

Originally the site of a Roman temple, the Cathedral was begun in 1163, the foundation stone being laid by Pope Alexander III. Work went on without interruption until its completion at the beginning of the 14th century. It must have been a huge task of coordination, though there were several instances of poor liaison: for example, the carvings for the main portal were completed 65 years before the doors were finished.

The Cathedral has been the scene of many historic occasions. In 1430 Henry VI of England was crowned there, and later Mary Stuart was married to François II. Henri IV was also married there to Margaret of Valois in 1572 but, being a protestant and therefore debarred entry, he had to wait outside while the ceremony was performed. During the Revolution many of the statues were destroyed as being 'offensive to Republican eyes'. For a time the building was used as a warehouse. Napoleon ordered the cathedral to be returned to its original religious function and it was here in 1804 that his coronation took place, with the Emperor snatching the crown from the pontiff and crowning first himself and then the Empress Josephine. After this the building gradually fell into disrepair.

The turning point came in 1840 with the publication of *The Hunchback of Notre Dame,* the romantic novel by Hugo, which so roused public opinion that the government ordered the building to be restored. The work was entrusted to Viollet-le-Duc, who for the next quarter of a century supervised the erection of the spire, the replacement of the stained glass and statues, and the addition of gargoyles to the exterior. His transformation of Notre Dame has been described as a work of genius, so faithfully did he recreate the original.

A climb up the 397 steep steps in the northwest tower entered from the Rue du Cloître on the north side of the cathedral (closed Tuesdays) gives an unequalled view of the Ile de la Cité and the Seine. Also in the Rue du Cloître is the Musée de Notre Dame (open at various times) containing documents, paintings and other objects illustrating the history of the cathedral.

 Off the Rue du Cloître is the Rue Chanoinesse, one of the oldest streets on the island, lined with ancient houses originally built for the canons. In the Square de l'Ile de France at the eastern end of the Ile de la Cité is a moving memorial to the 200,000 French people deported by the Germans in the last war. Linked to the Ile de la Cité by the traffic-free Pont St Louis dating from 1869, the Ile St Louis is bisected in an east-west direction by the narrow Rue St Louis en l'Ile, lined in places by fashionable restaurants. Encircled by peaceful shady *quais*, the island is one of the most tranquil places in Paris. Most of the houses, which fetch astronomically high prices on the open market, date from the 17th and 18th centuries.

Left of the Pont St Louis the Quai de Bourbon begins, continuing along the north side of the island as far as the Pont Marie, in use since 1635. Around the north east corner of the island, between the Pont Marie and the Pont Sully, is the Quai d'Anjou [8B5]. At its junction with the eastern end of the central Rue St Louis en l'Ile is the charming Hôtel Lambert, built in 1640, 'a house made for a king who would also be a philosopher', wrote Voltaire, who lived there for a time. Round the corner in the Quai d'Anjou is the celebrated Hôtel de Lauzun, an elegant mansion dating from 1658, where Baudelaire once lived. Owned by the municipality of Paris the house is used frequently for official receptions, though the magnificently decorated interior is open to visitors. In the house the members of the Club des Hachischins (hashish eaters) used to meet in 1845.

Nearly every house on the Quai d'Anjou bears a tablet commemorating someone or other who lived there.

5. Grands Boulevards

Following the line of the ancient fortifications which enclosed the northern part of the city from the 14th to the 18th century are some of the busiest traffic arteries of Paris, a network of tree-shaded boulevards forming a wedge with its tip touching the Etoile [1D3] and its base in line with the Rue de Richelieu and the Palais Royal [3F2]. The area is bounded on the north by the Boulevard Haussmann, named after the man who more than any other transformed the capital from an unhealthy town of narrow streets to a beautiful and spacious city.

When they were created in the 19th century the boulevards were a popular promenade of Parisians, and they are still lined with some of the most exclusive shops in the world.

The wide Avenue de Wagram strikes north from the Etoile [1D3] past the porcelain façade of the curious Ceramic Hotel to the Place des Ternes [2C4], noted for its flower market. The square marks the western terminus of the long Rue de Faubourg St Honoré, off which a short way east is the little Rue Daru, dominated by the 19th-century Russian Orthodox church (open in the mornings). In the Rue Berryer, farther along on the right, is the interesting Centre National d'Art Contemporaine, inaugurated in 1970, which stages temporary exhibitions. It occupies the ancient mansion where the French president Paul Doumer was assassinated in 1932.

At the point where the Rue du Faubourg St Honoré crosses the Boulevard Haussmann, the Rue Rembrandt leads north to the Parc de Monceau [2C5], ringed by a wealthy residential quarter. An attractive little park with a lake, it is decorated with statues of Gounod, Chopin, Maupassant, and others. The eastern exit is into the Avenue Velasquez, along which is the Musée Cernuschi [2C5], a small but valuable collection of early Chinese art (see p 61). Parallel with the Rue Velasquez on the south is the Rue de Monceau, in which is the Musée Nissim de Camondo [2C6], an annex of the Musée des Arts Décoratifs bequeathed by the Comte de Camondo in memory of his son Nissim, killed in the 1914-18 war. It is furnished throughout with 18th-century works of art.

In the Boulevard Haussmann east of its junction with the Rue du Faubourg St Honoré is the Musée Jacquemart André, with a magnificent art collection (see p 63). Beyond the Place Chassaigne Goyon, the Rue du Faubourg St Honoré, lined with fashionable shops, crosses the Place Beauvau to skirt the Palais de l'Elysée [2E6], occupied by French presidents in turn since 1873. The main reception rooms are superbly decorated in Louis XV and Louis XVI style. One of the many innovations introduced by President Giscard d'Estaing is that parts of the Elysée may be visited on Sunday mornings.

Adjoining the Elysée is the British Embassy, where Thackeray was married and Somerset Maugham born.

Beyond the American Embassy next door, the Rue du Faubourg St Honoré ends at its junction with the handsome Rue Royale, with its famous Edwardian restaurant of Maxim's, one of the most expensive in Paris, where evening dress is obligatory on Fridays. Dominating the vista of this and other streets converging on it is the huge and fashionable church of la Madeleine [3E1], begun in 1764, transformed by Napoleon in the style of a classical Greek temple, and only finally completed and consecrated in 1842. The view from the steps down the Rue Royale takes in the Place de la Concorde, the Seine, and the Palais Bourbon beyond.

The Place de la Madeleine, made colourful by a flower market, is bordered by boutiques and high-class food shops. Built in 1826 on the site of the old Madeleine cemetery, the Chapelle Expiatoire contains funeral monuments of Louis XVI by Bosio, and of Marie Antoinette by Cortot. The king and queen were originally buried in the cemetery along with thousands of others guillotined during the Revolution.

Running northeast from the Madeleine, the busy Boulevard de la Madeleine merges into the Boulevard des Capucines, most fashionable of all the boulevards, its name commemorating a convent that vanished long ago. The Musée Cognacq-Jay on the right [3E1] contains a fine collection of 18th-century works of art (see p 62), but more of a landmark is the Olympia, one of the few surviving old-style music halls in Paris. The Boulevard des Capucines crosses the Place de l'Opéra [3E2], dominated on the north by the enormous Opéra, the world's biggest theatre, in size if not in seating capacity. Twelve years in the building, the theatre was designed by Charles Garnier and completed in 1875. Its front, elaborately decorated with busts and groups of statuary, 'has no style', complained the empress Eugénie, 'being neither Greek nor Roman'. The architect explained that it was in fact the style of Napoleon III, her husband. Sumptuously decorated inside, the foyer and grand staircase provide an appropriate setting for the elite of Paris. With its entrance in the Place Charles Garnier, the Musée de l'Opéra contains busts, photographs and souvenirs of artists who have performed at the theatre (see p 65).

Always crowded, the Place de l'Opéra is bordered by big and small shops and the famous, impersonal, and expensive Café de la Paix. Most notable of the seven streets converging on it are the three on the south side. These are the Avenue de l'Opéra leading to the Palais Royal, the Rue du Quatre Septembre running east to the Bourse, and, most famous of all, the Rue de la Paix [3E1], lined with expensive perfumery and jewellers' shops and the top fashion houses. The Rue de la Paix crosses the Rue Daunou, in which is the famous Harry's Bar (see p 82).

At the far end of the Rue de la Paix is the elegant Place Vendôme. The houses bordering it, remarkable for their unity of style, were designed by Mansart, Louis XIV's favourite architect, in 1708. In the centre of the square is a column set up by Napoleon in 1810 to commemorate his victories over the Austrians and Germans, the main incidents of the battles being depicted in the bas-reliefs on its base. Around the square are luxury shops and the famous Ritz hotel.

North-east of the Place de l'Opéra the Boulevard des Capucines is continued by the Boulevard des Italiens, along which cinemas alternate with cafés and shops. Very much in vogue in the late 19th century, the street takes its name from the Italian opera singers who performed at the theatre which preceded the Opéra Comique, subsequently rechristened Salle Favart, the state theatre near its northern end. The theatre, the main elevation of which faces the tiny Place Boieledieu, now puts on more plays than comic opera.

On its way east, the Boulevard des Italiens is joined by the Boulevard Haussmann and ends at its junction with the Rue de Richelieu on one side and the Rue Drouot on the other. In the Hotel des Ventes in the Rue Drouot north of the intersection the main auctions of Paris used to be held most afternoons, when all kinds of objects came under the hammer. East of the junction is the short Boulevard Montmartre [3E3], on the left side of which is the Musée Grévin, the Paris equivalent of Madame Tussaud's (see p 62).

Extending on a north-south line between the Boulevard Haussmann and the Avenue de l'Opéra is the Rue de Richelieu, which skirts the west side of the huge Palais Royal [3F2], built in the 17th century by Cardinal Richelieu though much altered since. The garden, an oasis of calm amid the bustle of the surrounding streets, is enclosed by galleries built in 1781 and let out as fashionable shops, gambling houses, and cafés. In the Rue de Beaujolais, on the north side, is the Grand Véfour, the smallest top quality restaurant in France.

The southwest part of the Palais Royal is occupied by the Théâtre Français, opened in 1854 and fronted by two elegant fountains. It is the home of the Comédie Française, founded in 1680 and famed for its high standard of classical drama. Administered by the Beaux Arts, the company is made up of *sociétaires* who share in the profits and *pensionnaires* who get a salary and a fixed fee for each performance. Facing the theatre is the Civette, the oldest *tabac* in Paris, founded in 1820. From the square the Rue St Honoré, one of the oldest thoroughfares in Paris, leads west to its junction with the Rue Royale, beyond which it continues as the Rue du Faubourg St Honoré. At this end of the Rue St Honoré is the 17th-century church of St Roch [3F2], the finest example of baroque architecture in the city. Inside are some fine memorials, including a marble group near the altar. France's greatest dramatist, Corneille, is buried here.

Along the narrow Rue de Richelieu north of the Place André Malraux is the Bibliothèque Nationale [3E2], one of the largest libraries in the world.

A right turn into the Rue du Quatre Septembre off the Rue de Richelieu beyond the library leads to the Bourse or Stock Exchange [3E3], built in the style of a Roman temple. The Bourse is at its busiest from 12.30 to 14.30.

6. Right Bank

The narrow strip stretching east-west along the right bank of the Seine between the Place de la Concorde and the Place de la Bastille [8B6] is bounded on the north by the Rue de Rivoli and its continuation the Rue St Antoine. Elegant and dignified on the west, animated and popular on the east, the area contains many historic sights. But few of them are near the Seine from which, like the local fishermen, tourists have been driven by the *voie express* or expressway running along this side of the river.

Adjoining the Place de la Concorde on the east are the Tuileries Gardens [3F1], laid out in 1664 by the celebrated landscape architect Le Nôtre. Protected from the Seine and the expressway alongside it by long terraces, their chestnut groves, lawns and flower beds are decorated with statues, fountains, and ponds. At each end of the terrace dominating the Place de la Concorde are the Jeu de Paume – once the tennis court of the long-since-demolished Tuileries palace and now an important picture gallery – and the Orangerie, used for temporary exhibitions. Dividing the gardens at their eastern end from the buildings of the Louvre is the busy Avenue du Général Lemonnier, beyond which is the site of the Tuileries palace, the only reminders of which are the two square pavilions closing the long wings of the Louvre. The 16th-century palace took its name from the tile kilns that previously occupied the site. The Arc de Triomphe du Carrousel which once formed the entrance to the palace courtyard was built by Napoleon in 1808 to mark his campaign victories, and is modelled on the larger arch at the Etoile. On the other side of the arch is the Place du Carrousel [3F2], where Napoleon reviewed regiments of his Grande Armée.

The buildings on either side of the square were built by Napoleon III in 1852. One forms the main entrance to the galleries of the Louvre. From the Place du Carrousel the view extends the length of the Tuileries Gardens and along the Avenue des Champs Elysées as far as the Arc de Triomphe, almost two miles away.

Its unity of style unimpaired by having been added to at different times, the huge complex of the Louvre consists of the Vieux Louvre on the east, enclosing the Cour Carré; the Nouveau Louvre in the centre, built in the 19th century on either side of the Place du Carrousel, and continuing on the west by two long wings joining up with the Pavillons de Flore and Marsan. The national art collections of the Musée du Louvre are the biggest and most valuable ever housed in any one building (see p 64). In the north-west wing of the complex is the Musée des Arts Décoratifs, entered from the Rue de Rivoli and showing the developments of artistic taste through the ages (see p 60).

Facing the majestic 17th-century colonnade designed by Claude Perrault on the far side of the Place du Louvre is the parish church of St Germain l'Auxerrois, dedicated to St Germain of Auxerre and dating from the 12th century. Its flamboyant west front adjoins the *mairie* or town hall of the district. Between the two is a high belfry, housing a 35-bell carillon that plays three old French tunes. Less cheerful was the signal rung from the bell tower on the night of 24 August 1572 for the St Bartholomew massacre of the Huguenots.

Running east from the Louvre is the Rue de Rivoli, one of the great lateral arteries of Paris named by Napoleon after one of his victories in Italy. The western part of the street was built by Napoleon I, the eastern by Napoleon III. That part of the street bordering the Tuileries Gardens is flanked by the imposing façades of classical mansions, with covered pavements, high-class shops, and several luxury hotels.

After crossing the Rue du Pont Neuf the Rue de Rivoli skirts the Place du Châtelet [7A3], the main junction on the great north-south traffic artery formed by the boulevards of Sébastopol, Palais, and St Michel. The Square is bordered by the Théâtre de la Ville (the former Théâtre Sarah Bernhardt) and the Théâtre du Châtelet, famed for its operettas. Dominating the north-east corner of the square is the fine 16th-century Tour St Jacques, sole surviving part of a church destroyed at the Revolution. East of the Place du Châtelet the Avenue Victoria named in honour of the queen's visit to the capital in 1854, leads to the vast renaissance-style Hôtel de Ville [8A4], the town hall of Paris. The wide square fronting the building, now the Place de l'Hôtel de Ville, was the scene of public executions from the 14th to the end of the 18th century.

Prolonging the Rue de Rivoli on the east, the Rue St Antoine, which follows the line of the old Roman road from Paris to Melun, has a much more popular character, being animated and noisy for much of the day. On the south side of the street is the Temple Ste Marie, designed by Mansart and roofed with a cupola.

In the area bounded by the Rue de Rivoli, Rue St Antoine and the Seine is an ancient Jewish quarter, still medieval in aspect, which was saved from the bulldozer only by the vigorous protests of a group of conservationists called Les Amis du Vieux Paris. Behind the Hôtel de Ville the classic façade of the church of St Gervais – St Protais fronts on the Place St Gervais, shaded by an enormous elm planted in memory of the tree under which in medieval times the city fathers settled disputes. From the square the Rue François Miron, lined in places by old mansions entered through courtyards, crosses the Rue Geoffroy l'Asnier leading down to the Seine. At the junction of this street and the Rue du Grenier sur l'Eau is the Memorial du Martyr Juif Inconnu, placed there in 1956 in memory of the many Jews who vanished in the concentration camps of Nazi Germany. A building nearby, decorated with the cross of David, houses the Jewish information centre of Paris.

The Rue de l'Hôtel de Ville crosses the southern end of the Rue Geoffroy l'Asnier and continues east to its junction with the Rue du Figuier and the Rue Fauconnier. In the Rue du Figuier is the Hôtel de Sens, a medieval manor once the residence of the archbishops of Sens.

At the eastern end of the Rue St Antoine is the large and melancholy Place de la Bastille [8B6]. It occupies the site of the infamous Bastille prison, destroyed by the Parisians on July 14 1789. The building was used as a royal treasury in the reign of Henri IV then until its destruction in 1789, as a state prison. It takes a high-powered imagination to evoke its history as the flashpoint of the Revolution. On the façade of one of the buildings at the edge of the square is a plan of the fortress and set in the pavement are white stones marking the lines of the walls.

7. Gare du Nord, Montmartre

Adjoining the Gare du Nord on the west is the sandy ridge occupied by the old village of Montmartre, invaded by hordes of sightseers from noon to midnight in season. Its steep narrow streets are usually written off as a tourist trap yet their rustic charm survives, particularly in spring and autumn. Even in summer, the splendid views of Paris from the terrace of the Sacré Coeur [3B3] basilica alone justify the journey.

A short walk from the Gare du Nord [4C4], the Boulevard de Magenta leads north to its junction with the Boulevard Rochechouart. North again is the Porte de Clignancourt [3A3], of interest if only for its vast Marché aux Puces or flea market. Lined with antique shops, the Rue la Fayette cuts diagonally southwest across the Boulevard de Magenta and, a short way on, the Place Liszt [4D4]. South of this square is the Rue de Paradis, a street given over to the making and selling of tableware. It provides an appropriate setting for the Musée de Baccarat, a fascinating collection of crystal (see p 60).

Farther on, the Rue la Fayette crosses the Rue du Faubourg Montmartre, which leads on the left to the Rue Richer [3D3] and the celebrated Folies Bergère, 'the best-dressed nude revue in Paris'. West of its junction with the Boulevard de Magenta [4B4], the Boulevard Rochechouart and its continuation the Boulevard de Clichy crosses the Place Pigalle [3C2] and the Place Blanche [3B2] as it skirts the southern edge of the *butte* or hill of Montmartre. With their restaurants, *dancings*, cabarets, and strip clubs spilling out into the adjoining streets, these two squares are the centre of a neon-lit and mainly sleazy night life. One historic landmark in the Place Blanche is the famous Bal du Moulin Rouge, opened in 1889 and still generating an atmosphere of the 'gay Nineties'. In its heyday all Paris, along with the prince of Wales (the future Edward VII) and his entourage, came to applaud the girls, immortalized by Toulouse-Lautrec, who danced the can-can to the stirring sounds of Offenbach's music.

Crowning a hill 300ft above the level of the Seine, the village of Montmartre – annexed by Paris in 1860 – still has remnants of the vineyards that once ringed it round. It is named (Mons Martyrum) as the place where St Denis, 3rd-century apostle and first bishop of Paris, was martyred with his two companions by the Romans. Crowning the *butte* is one of the traditional sights of Paris, the great white basilica of Sacré Coeur [3B3], surrounded by picturesque narrow streets once lived in by artists and bohemians but now sadly commercialized.

The first to occupy a studio in the then-peaceful village at the turn of the century was Renoir. He was soon followed by Utrillo, Dufy, Gauguin, Modigliani, and others, who were joined in turn by anarchists and other eccentrics of little talent. There are two ways to get to Montmartre: by a stiff climb up a series of steep streets and stone staircases, or by the funicular operating day and night from the *gare inférieure* in the Rue de Steinkerque off the Boulevard Rochechouart (métro: Anvers).

The terminus of the funicular is close by the basilica of Sacré Coeur which was conceived as a votive offering for the ending of the Franco-Prussian war of 1870-1871, paid for with donations from all over the country and built in the romanesque-byzantine style characteristic of southern France. Building began in 1873, but the church was not consecrated until 1919. Entered by a porch flanked by statues of St Louis and Joan of Arc, the interior – dark and crowded with pilgrims most of the time – is notable for its stained glass, mosaics, and statuary. Rising above the 270ft high dome is the campanile housing the great 19-ton Savoyarde bell. A tiring climb up the 350 steps in the dome (closed from 12.00 to 14.00) leads to galleries from which there is a great circular panorama, though the view from the terrace fronting the church is almost as impressive, particularly at dusk when the lights of Paris start to come on.

In contrast to the Sacré Coeur is the modest little church of St Pierre de Montmartre between the basilica and the Place du Tertre on the west [3B3]. Consecrated in 1147, it has an interesting interior, with corbelled columns in the nave and rib vaulting above the choir.

The original aspect of old Montmartre is preserved in the narrow streets west and north of the Place du Tertre, the old village square, haunted by aspiring artists and bordered by restaurants. Running north from the Place du Tertre is the Rue du Mont Cenis (so steep it is named after an alpine pass), off which are the Rue St Rustique (the main street of the village in the 17th century) and the Rue St Vincent, with the Musée du Vieux Montmartre (see p 66). Parallel with the Rue du Mont Cenis on the west is the Rue des Saules, with the tourist office at the southern end, and the celebrated Lapin-Agile café-bar (once a regular meeting place of writers and poets) and the Cimetière St Vincent at the northern.

The village is bounded on the north and west by the Rue Caulaincourt and the Rue Custine. Entered from the Rue Caulaincourt is the peaceful cemetery of Montmartre [3B2], opened in 1825 and officially known as the Cimetière du Nord. Among the famous people buried in the cemetery are Zola, Théophile Gautier, Berlioz, Dumas, Offenbach, the Goncourt brothers, and Nijinsky.

8. Les Halles and the Marais

Still known by the great market that regulated its way of life until it was moved to the outskirts several years ago, the old and densely populated artisan quarter of Les Halles north of the Rue de Rivoli contrasts sharply with the once-aristocratic Marais district adjoining it on the east. Taking its name from the great marsh reclaimed by the Knights Templars on which it is built, the Marais is a veritable museum of 17th-century French domestic architecture. Happily this was recognized by André Malraux in 1962 and many of its ancient *hôtels particuliers* or mansions have now been protected or tastefully restored.

From the east side of the Place de la Bourse [3E3] the Rue Notre Dame des Victoires runs south across the busy Rue Réaumur to the church founded by Louis XIII in 1628 to mark the capture of La Rochelle from the Huguenots.

Over the years the church of Notre Dame des Victoires has become associated with deliverance from danger on land or sea, and the interior is decorated with some 30,000 *ex votos*. Behind the church is the elegant circular Place des Victoires [3F2], centred on a statue of Louis XIV. On the far side of the square is the Rue Croix des Petits Champs, off which the Rue Coquillière leads east to the site of Les Halles [3F3], central food market of Paris until moved to Rungis, near Orly airport, a few years ago. Protected from the weather by huge steel and glass umbrellas, full of bustle and noise at night, asleep by day, it dominated the life of the surrounding streets. Described by Zola as the 'belly of Paris', Les Halles was the in place for fashionable Parisians to rub shoulders with porters and journeymen in the early morning as they ate their onion soup in one of the bistrots around the market.

The market area between the Bourse and the Boulevard de Sébastopol has been cleared to make way for a vast project due to be completed in 1983. The main feature will be a park of 6 hectares at street level and shops and exhibition halls, discos and sports centres, metro and post office below ground.

Parallel with the Boulevard de Sébastopol, the popular Rue St Denis is the Kings Road of Paris, in which strip clubs and places dealing in erotica alternate with antique and curio shops.

In the Rue Rambuteau off the Rue St Denis to the north is the 16th-century church of St Eustache [3F3], its interior decorated with frescoes and statuary a happy blend of late gothic and early renaissance. Farther north the Rue Etienne Marcel crosses the wide Rue Turbigo. From the junction of the two streets the Rue Pierre Lescot leads south past what used to be the east side of Les Halles to the Square des Innocents, once an ancient burial ground, with gardens centred on the beautiful renaissance Fontaine des Innocents.

Across the wide and busy Boulevard de Sébastopol is the Marais district, the stately houses lining the Rue de Quincampoix being typical of the condition of many others in nearby streets before restoration. In the Hôtel de Beaufort in the Rue de Quincampoix the Scot John Law set up his banking house in 1716, and when his Mississippi company crashed it brought ruin to thousands.

Parallel with the Boulevard de Sébastopol is the Rue St Martin, one of the oldest thoroughfares in Europe. With its continuation the Rue St Jacques on the south side of the Seine, it follows the line of the old Roman road to Orléans, trod for centuries by pilgrims on their way to the shrine of Santiago de Compostella in northern Spain.

Between the Rue St Martin and the Rue Beaubourg is the plateau Beaubourg dominated by the art and cultural centre officially named after the late president Georges Pompidou but more popularly known as the Centre Beaubourg [8A4], a vast steel and glass structure. Along with the Musée National d'Art Moderne it incorporates a library, meeting halls, children's workshop and information bureaux geared to the needs of young people. The centre is open Mon, Wed, Thurs and Fri 1200 to 2200, Sat and Sun 1000 to 2200.

Hemmed in by houses in the Rue St Martin nearby is the flamboyant Gothic church of St Merri, part 16th century, with some fine stained glass windows. North along the same street is the Conservatoire des Arts et Métiers [4E/F4], partly housed in the Cluniac priory of St Martin des Champs (see p 60).

Crossing the Rue St Martin, the long Rue Réaumur leads east past the offices of the newspaper *France Soir* to the Square du Temple [4F5], where Louis XVI and his family were imprisoned in a tower once part of a powerful *commanderie* of the Knights Templars, from which the square gets its name. From here the king was taken to the guillotine on January 21 1793, the queen to the Conciergerie on August 2. The tower was pulled down a long time ago and has been replaced by a garden.

The Rue du Temple skirting the west side of the square leads north to the Place de la République [4E5], passing the classical façade of the 17th-century church of Ste Elizabeth, containing finely worked woodcarvings originally in Arras cathedral. The Rue de Bretagne runs east from the south side of the Square du Temple to its junction with the Rue Vieille du Temple [4F5]. Parallel with this street on the west is the Rue des Archives. At their southern end the two streets cross the Rue des Francs Bourgeois, which borders on the south the Archives Nationales [8A5]. Entered from the Rue des Francs Bourgeois the palatial building houses the national archives and the small but interesting Musée de L'Histoire de France (see p 63).

West along the Rue des Francs Bourgeois (free burghers exempt from municipal taxes) are several imposing town houses and at No 55 the cynically named Monte de Piété or municipal pawnshop. East along the street is the renaissance mansion of the Hôtel Carnavalet [8A5], enlarged by Mansart in the 17th century and containing the remarkable Musée Carnavalet illustrating the history of Paris (see p 61). On the other side of the street is the late 16th-century Hôtel Lamoignon, one of the grandest mansions in the Marais, occupied by the Bibliotheque Historique de la Ville de Paris. A short way on is the Rue Payenne, with the Temple de la Religion de L'Humanité founded in 1903 by the Positivist church of Brazil. Prolonging the Rue Payenne on the other side of the Rue des

Francs Bourgeois is the Rue Pavée, one of the first streets in Paris to have a pavement. At the eastern end of the Rue des Francs Bourgeois, within the triangle formed by the Rue St Antoine and the Boulevard Beaumarchais is one of the most elegant squares in Paris, the monumental Place des Vosges [8B6]. Created by the gay Gascon Henri IV in the early 17th century, it is bordered by identical classical façades rising above arcades.

Once known as the Place Royale, the square was renamed in 1792 in acknowledgement of the help given to the Revolutionary cause by the *département* or county of the Vosges. Victor Hugo lived for 16 years in an apartment in the Hôtel d'Arnaud (No 6) and the house is now converted into a museum containing relics of the writer.

Filling the space between the Place des Vosges and the Rue St Antoine, to the south, is the elegant and interesting Hôtel de Sully, bought in 1634 by the Duc de Sully, zealous finance minister of Henri IV. Inside is an information centre giving details of the history of the Marais and its restoration.

9. Faubourg St Germain, Luxembourg, Montparnasse

The elongated district extending south from the left bank of the Seine changes from palatial to popular and finally, at Maine-Montparnasse [6c6], to ultra-modern.

Across the Seine from the Louvre is the Institut de France [7A2], a domed building designed by Le Vau in 1672 to house the college founded by Cardinal Mazarin for the youth of the newly won provinces of Alsace, Flanders, and the Roussillon. Since 1805 it has been the headquarters of five academies, the Académie Française, Belles Lettres, Sciences, Beaux Arts, and Sciences Morales et Politiques. Most famous is the Académie Française, founded in 1629. Inside the building is the sumptuously decorated library of the cardinal, the Bibliothèque Mazarine.

Adjoining the Institut on the east is the Hôtel des Monnaies or Mint, with its interesting workshops (open to visitors) where coins and medals are struck. In the building is the Musée Monétaire, an absorbing collection of coins, medals and seals (see p 65).

A short way west is the 19th-century Ecole des Beaux Arts [7A2], where the fine arts are taught to students of all nationalities. Entered from the Rue Bonaparte, the court of honour contains such architectural relics as the doorway of the 16th century Château d'Anet, one-time home of Henri II's mistress Diane de Poitiers, and the main façade of the Château de Gaillon, also of the 16th century. Most of the shops in the Rue Bonaparte sell books, paintings, and antiques. The street passes the short Rue des Beaux Arts (with the house in which Oscar Wilde died destitute in 1900) before reaching the *place* dominated by the ancient church of St Germain des Près [7B2], founded along with the abbey of which it formed part by St Germain of Autun, 6th-century bishop of Paris. Though the church has been many times restored, the romanesque tower and nave are little different from when they were built in the 11th century. In the nave are the astonishing frescoes painted in the 19th century by Hippolyte Flandrin, and near the sacristy is a monument to Lord James Douglas, commander of Louis XIII's Scottish bodyguard, killed in battle at Douai in 1645. Nearby is the tomb of René Descartes, the 17th-century philosopher.

The Place St Germain des Près, lively at any time of day, is ringed by cafés and night clubs. One of the institutions of the quarter is the Café de Flore, its terrace a popular place for watching the passing scene. Its rival nearby is the famous Café des Deux Magots, where Jean Paul Sartre and Simone de Beauvoir met to discuss their existentialist philosophy.

Created by Haussmann, the Boulevard St Germain runs west from the square to bisect the Faubourg St Germain, once the most aristocratic district of Paris, its streets still lined with elegant town houses and mansions fronted by monumental gateways and courtyards. Most are now occupied by government ministries and embassies. Streets which have best preserved their 18th-century residential character are the Rues de Lille, Varenne, and Grenelle. The splendid Hôtel de Matignon in the Rue de Varenne [6A/B6] adjoins the largest private park in Paris.

From the Place St Germaine des Près the Rue Bonaparte runs south to pass near the Place St Sulpice [7B2], with the imposing Fontaine des Quatre Evêques, commemorating the four bishops of Fénélon, Bossuet, Flechier, and Massillon. The majestic interior of the vast and severely classical church of St Sulpice is decorated with superb murals painted by Delacroix.

The Rue Bonaparte ends at the Rue de Vaugirard, the longest street in Paris, which stretches for nearly three miles all the way from the Boulevard St Michel to the Porte de Versailles and the adjoining Parc des Expositions, scene of the annual Paris motor show.

East of the junction of the two streets is the Petit Luxembourg [7C2], an official residence, and the Palais du Luxembourg, the handsome seat of the Conseil de la Republique or senate. Built in 1620 for Marie de Medicis, widow of Henri IV, on land previously owned by the Duc de Luxembourg, the palace was the headquarters of the Luftwaffe during the German occupation of 1940-44.

Backing onto the palace are the Luxembourg Gardens, probably the most beautiful in Paris, with their fine views, groups of statuary, trees, and flower beds. Laid out by de Brosse in the Italian style, they have a recognizably French atmosphere. With their donkey rides, puppet shows, and round pond for sailing boats, no gardens in Paris are more popular with children.

Facing the Palais du Luxembourg on the north side of the Rue de Vaugirard is the Odéon [7c2], a state theatre now linked with the Comédie Française and famed for its popular arcades at street level.

In the Rue de l'Ancienne Comédie [7B2] on the far side of the Boulevard St Germain is the historic Café la Procope, founded in 1689 by the Sicilian Procopio Cultelli, where Talleyrand and Robespierre met during the Revolution. Off the Rue de Vaugirard west of the Odéon is the Rue de Tournon, with the Café de Tournon, the favourite meeting place of American writers after the last war, and the house where Paul Jones, the Scot who commanded a squadron of French ships against the English, died in 1792. In the same year over a hundred priests were massacred during the Terror in the church of St Joseph de Carmes, farther west in the Rue de Vaugirard.

Half a mile on, the Rue de Vaugirard crosses the wide Boulevard Raspail [7c1], the southern end of which intersects the Boulevard du Montparnasse. Around the animated square formed by the intersection, the heart of the old quarter, are the famous cafés of the Dôme, Coupole and Rotonde (métro: Vavin). Until they fell out, Lenin and Trotsky frequently met in the Dôme, founded in 1897, a time when the artists and writers of Montparnasse were much the same as Puccini portrayed them in his opera *La Bohème*. At the vast Coupole some years later Hemingway and Scott Fitzgerald often drank everyone else under the table. A few yards along from the Rotonde is the Select, another 'literary' café still popular with writers. At this end of the Boulevard Raspail is Rodin's famous statue of Balzac. West along the Boulevard du Montparnasse, beyond the ancient church of Notre Dame des Champs, is the Place du 18 juin 1940. Extending south from the square and incorporating a new station in place of the old Gare Montparnasse is the ultra-modern development of Maine-Montparnasse, a vast commercial centre topped by a tower nearly 700 ft high. On the 56th floor, reached by lift in 35 seconds, is the highest restaurant in Europe, built on three levels so that every diner has a panoramic view of Paris.

West of the new centre is the Rue Antoine Bourdelle, in which the workshops of the sculptor house the Musée Antoine Bourdelle (see p 61).

Adjoining the Boulevard Raspail south of its junction with the Boulevard du Montparnasse is the Cimetière du Sud [7E1], popularly known as the cemetery of Montparnasse, interesting for its tombs if not for its setting. Among the celebrities buried there are Baudelaire, Maupassant, and Saint-Saens.

10. Left Bank

Centred on the ancient university of the Sorbonne and bounded on the north by the Seine, the Left Bank is the vibrant student quarter of Paris and one of the oldest parts of the city. Cosmopolitan and noisy near the river, more relaxed in the south, it contains many historic sights and several distinct localities, each different in atmosphere. On the south side of the Pont St Michel linking the Il de la Cité with the left bank of the Seine is the Place St Michel [7B3], dominated by the 55 ft high Fontaine St Michel, built by Davioud in 1860 and topped by a bronze group by Duret depicting the saint slaying the dragon.

Created in the 1850's by Haussmann, Prefect of Paris in the reign of Napoleon III, the Boulevard St Michel (Boul'Mich) runs south from the Place St Michel to bisect the student quarter as it climbs gently up to its junction with the Boulevard Montparnasse. One of the main traffic arteries of the Left Bank, it changes in character along its length, the northern end staying lively until the small hours, the southern end, more residential and institutional, remaining deserted after dark.

Left off the boulevard the Rue St Séverin forms part of the picturesque small quarter of St Séverin. Made up at the most of five or six narrow streets with names derived from the signs that identified them to the illiterate in medieval times, the district is noted for its inexpensive small restaurants of all nationalities, and its cosmopolitan population. The quarter is centred on the church of St Séverin, named after a hermit said to have miraculously healed the Frankish king Clovis, and probably the best example of flamboyant Gothic in the whole of Paris, rich in finely carved stonework and old glass.

Bounded by the Quai de Montébello and the Boulevard St Germain, the Quartier Maubert ('le vieux Maube') prolonging St Séverin on the east is equally medieval in character, its maze of narrow streets being derived from what it once was – a group of walled vineyards. From the Place Maubert [8C4], with its colourful street market, the quarter extends east behind the Quai de la Tournelle and

south-east along the Rue Monge as far as the church of
St Nicolas de Chardonnet, a mixture of architectural styles
of different periods. Off the Boulevard St Germain near the
Place Maubert is the Rue des Anglais, so called because of
the many English students attending the Sorbonne
who lived there in medieval times. South along the Rue
Monge are the Arènes de Lutèce, excavated in the 19th
century and laid out as a garden. Dating from the 2nd or
3rd centuries and seating some 10,000 people, the arena
was destroyed by barbarian invaders around 280.

The Rue du Puits de l'Ermite, off the Rue Monge a short
way on, crosses the Place du Puits de l'Ermite to the
Institut Musulman, topped by a slender minaret.
Adjoining a mosque are Turkish baths, a bazaar selling arts
and crafts of North Africa, and a café serving Arab food.
The mosque, built in 1926, is open to visitors from 10.00 to
12.00 and 14.00 to 17.00 every day except Wednesday.

Behind the mosque is the Jardin des Plantes [8D5], entered
from the Rue Buffon. Originally a royal herb garden, it was
converted by the famous naturalist Buffon into a botanical
garden combined with a natural history museum. A
menagerie was added in 1793. It is now a pleasant park,
with a variety of statuary, impeccably maintained flower
beds and some fine old trees, each of which is labelled. A
separate charge is made for entry to every enclosure. The
botanical gardens proper contain over 20,000 different
species of plants.

At the junction of the Rue Buffon and the Rue Geoffroy
St Hilaire is the fascinating Musée d'Histoire Naturelle
spanning three million years of human adventure (see p 63).

Behind the Gare d'Austerlitz [8D5/6] south-east of the
Jardin des Plantes is the vast and severely styled Hôpital de
la Salpetrière, one of the main hospitals of Paris which
takes its name from the gunpowder works founded on the
site in 1656 by Louis XIV. In 1657 a hostel was built there
for the thousands of vagrants and outcasts then entrenched
around the Place de la Nation across the river. In 1678
Louis XIV ordered the building to be used to confine
'undisciplined women and girls'. It later became a lunatic
asylum, with the inmates chained to the walls, then a

prison. In the hospital grounds is a curious domed church built in the form of a Greek cross which can hold 4,000 people.

The Boulevard Vincent Auriol skirts the hospital on the south. It leads on the west to the wide Place d'Italie [8F4], off which is the wide and busy Avenue des Gobelins. Behind a modern façade on the left side of the avenue is the ancient Manufacture des Gobelins [8E4], state-owned but still named after its Flemish founders, the dyers Jean and Philibert Gobelin. World-famous for its high warp tapestry, it also has workshops producing the Beauvais (low warp) weave. Many of the tapestries are surprisingly modern, being woven to the designs of such artists as Chagall, Lurçat and others. Visitors to the workshops (open Wednesday, Thursday and Friday from 14.00 to 16.00) can watch the weavers using over 10,000 shades of silk and wool, the average worker creating with the patience of times past little over a square yard a year. A museum in the building contains specimens of tapestry and carpets of all periods, including some designed by Matisse. The Boulevard du Port Royal, off the Avenue des Gobelins on the north, skirts the huge Val de Grace military hospital [7E3], once a Benedictine convent founded by Anne of Austria, wife of Louis XIII, in gratitude for the birth in 1638 of the child that was to become Louis XIV – after 21 years of trying for an heir. The church of the convent, built in 1652, is famed for its majestic dome (one of the highest in Paris), covered inside with over 200 figures larger than life-size painted by Mignard. The convent buildings house the Musée de Service de Santé, which groups together paintings, documents, and other exhibits illustrating the development of caring for the wounded.

East off the Rue Claude Bernard fronting the hospital is the Rue de l'Arbalète, which crosses the Rue Mouffetard near the curious church of St Médard [8D4], beside the old Roman road to Lyon. The picturesque Rue Mouffetard, usually abbreviated to 'Mouffe', is well known for its morning food market. Prolonging the street on the north is the Place de la Contrescarpe [8D4], at the junction of the Rue Lacépède, ringed by some of the oldest streets in

Paris and one of the liveliest squares on the Left Bank, with many inexpensive resturants that stay open late.

From the square the Rue Blainville and its continuation the Rue de l'Estrapade lead west to the big Lycée Henri IV, the Bibliothèque Ste Geneviève, a 19th-century building housing the library of an abbey founded in 1624, and, fronting on the Place du Panthéon, the great cruciform Panthéon [7c3], with its immense dome, the 'Westminster Abbey of France', where the most famous Frenchmen are buried. Built as a church in the late 18th century, it was transformed by Napoleon into a temple of fame. Inside, on the walls of the huge hall, are painted scenes from the life of Ste Geneviève, patron saint of Paris, and from the Revolution. Those buried in the vaults (shown on conducted tours) include Victor Hugo, Voltaire, Zola, and Rousseau. A more interesting church is the nearby St Etienne du Mont, a charming blend of gothic plan and renaissance detail. Dating from the late 16th century, it has a spacious interior notable for its elaborate rood loft and its gilded chapel housing the shrine of Ste Geneviève, which still attracts pilgrims.

At the far end of the Rue Cujas leading off the square is the immense rectangle occupied by the Sorbonne [7c3] the central part of the University of Paris. The complex of buildings are made up mostly of the faculties of letters and science. The Sorbonne originated as a theological college founded in 1252 by Robert de Sorbon, confessor to St Louis, which gave its name to the faculty of theology and later to the whole university. Parts of the building are open to visitors and posted up in the entrance hall are dates and times of the lectures given there and in the nearby Collège de France. In the great hall is the famous mural of the Sacred Grove painted by Puvis de Chavannes. The domed church of the Sorbonne, facing the Place de la Sorbonne on the west, was begun by order of Richelieu in 1635 and contains the tomb of the cardinal, designed by Girardin, and paintings by Philippe de Champaigne in the dome.

Northwest, at the junction of the Boulevard St Michel and the Boulevard St Germain, is the magnificent Hôtel de Cluny [7b3], a Gothic mansion built for the abbots of the

The domed Church of the Sorbonne

Benedictine monastery at Cluny in Burgundy. Inside is a room called La Chambre de la Reine Blanche, lived in by Marie d'Angleterre, widow of Louis XII, white being the traditional colour of mourning for the queens of France. In the garden facing the Boulevard St Michel are the ruined Thermes or Roman baths, built in the 2nd century. Dating from the late 15th century, the mansion also houses the celebrated Musée de Cluny, one of the finest collections of medieval domestic and religious art (see p 62). The entrance to the museum is in the Place Paul Painlevé.

11. Invalides

Dominated on the west by the Eiffel Tower and bounded on the north by the Seine, the extensive district of the Invalides, with its classical façades and spacious vistas, is the most monumental part of Paris. In line with the Tuileries on the opposite bank of the Seine, the Quai Anatole France skirts the Gare d'Orsay, and beyond it the Palais de la Légion d'Honneur [7A1]. Founded by Napoleon in 1802 for military men and civilians alike, the order is divided into five classes, though all members wear the same miniature red rosette in their buttonholes. A newly-added wing houses the interesting Musée de la Légion d'Honneur (see p 64).

Facing the Pont de la Concorde [2F6] (symbolically resting on stone taken from the rubble of the Bastille) is the colonnaded façade of the Palais Bourbon [2F6], an 18th-century building with its original frontage in the Rue de l'Université, the side facing the river being a later addition. Since 1815 this has been the seat of the lower house of parliament, now called the Assemblée Nationale. In the last war the Germans made it their military headquarters for the Paris region.

The Quai d'Orsay, which starts on the far side of the bridge, skirts the front of the French foreign office, the name of one being synonymous with the other. Next to it is the neo-classic Gare des Invalides [2F5], with fast trains to Versailles. Forming part of the station is the Aérogare des Invalides, point of arrival and departure for those travelling to and from the airports of Orly and Roissy-en-France.

The Rue de Bourgogne links the Place du Palais Bourbon, behind the palace, with the Rue de Varenne [6A6], passing several government ministries. The Rue las Cases on the left leads to the neo-Gothic church of Ste Clotilde [6A6], where the composer César Franck (1822-90) was organist for over 30 years. In the Rue de Grenelle beyond the church is the pretty Fontaine des Quatre Saisons, designed by Bouchardon and decorated with bas-reliefs depicting the four seasons.

Set in a beautiful garden at the western end of the Rue de Varenne is the Hôtel Biron [6B6], a fine 18th-century building designed by Gabriel and once occupied by the aristocratic convent of Sacré Coeur. It houses the delightful Musée Rodin, a complete collection in originals or casts of the work of the sculptor Auguste Rodin (1840-1917), who had his studio here (see p 66).

The Rue de Varenne ends at the Boulevard des Invalides, which runs north then swings round to pass the main entrance of the massive Hôtel des Invalides [6A5], founded

The Hôtel des Invalides – a home for disabled soldiers

in the 17th century by Louis XIV as a home for disabled soldiers.

The vast expanse extending from the front of the building to the Seine is the Esplanade des Invalides, laid out in 1720. The buildings on either side of the imposing courtyard (the Cour du Dôme) on the south side of the complex contain the Musée de l'Armée (see p 60).

On the south side of the courtyard is the Dôme des Invalides and the Musée des Plans-Reliefs, an interesting collection of old models of fortified towns (see p 65). The gilded Dôme des Invalides, 320ft high, was built as a *chapelle royale* in 1675. The dominant feature of the interior is the quartzite and granite tomb of Napoleon, whose body was transferred here from St Helena in 1840. In the side chapels are the tombs of Napoleon's two brothers and of his son, along with those of Marshal Foch and the great military architect Vauban. Steps each side of the altar lead down to the crypt.

Behind the Dôme is the church of St Louis, hung with flags and decorated with memorials of Napoleon. Adjoining the semi-circular Place Vauban [6B5] facing the entrance to the Dôme des Invalides, the Avenue de Tourville leads to the Ecole Militaire [6B4], a military academy founded by Louis XV in 1773. It houses the staff colleges of the three military services.

Behind, in the Place de Fontenoy, is the huge Y-shaped Unesco building built in 1955-58 and decorated inside and out by famous artists: Henry Moore, Picasso, Lurçat, and others.

Extending from the majestic façade of the Ecole Militaire, fronted by an equestrian statue of Marshal Foch, is the former parade ground of the Champ de Mars (field of Mars, god of war). It stretches north-west for over half a mile to the Eiffel Tower [5A3], on the left bank of the Seine. Built to the design of engineer Gustave Eiffel for the exhibition set up on the Champ de Mars in 1889, the 1,050 ft high all-steel tower that bears his name has become a symbol of Paris. In its first year over 30 million people visited the tower, one of whom was that greatest of francophiles the future Edward VII. A tortuous stairway goes to the top but most people take the *ascenseurs* or lifts. The first stops at platform I, with its expensive restaurant, then continues to its terminus, platform II. Here there is often an hour-long queue for the second lift, which climbs to a narrow glassed-in ledge, from which another lift makes the ascent to the top – where there is a choice between making the windy climb to the upper deck or buying a well earned drink or a franked postcard.

The enormous view from the top extends in clear weather over a radius of nearly 50 miles, but the second platform is a better vantage point for picking out specific landmarks. The tower stays open after dark from May to October (métro: Trocadéro).

12. Museums

The world-famous Louvre apart, Paris has over forty museums. They cover not only painting and sculpture but a variety of other subjects, from coins and stamps to natural history and scientific invention. Some group priceless works of art in the delightfully appropriate setting of a 17th or 18th-century mansion. Many close for one or two days a week and on public holidays (Jan 1, May 1, July 14, Aug 15, Nov 1 and Dec 25). Admission charges can be high by our standards though there are usually reductions for students. Admission to some places is free at any time, to many others on Sundays.

Armée Hôtel des Invalides, 7e [6A5]. Not only war and its horrors but also the art and inventions it inspired. Well arranged exhibits include Viking swords, the bullet that killed Turenne, Napoleon's grey redingote, and a diorama of the Normandy landings. Open daily 10.00-18.00 (17.00 winter). Charge for entry covers the adjoining Dôme (Napoleon's tomb) and the Musée des Plans-Reliefs. *Métro:* Invalides.

Arts Africains 296 Avenue Daumesnil, 12e [off 8C6]. African works of art, including statues, paintings, and mythological masks, plus great aquarium with tortoises and crocodiles. Open daily except Tue 09.45-11.55 and 13.00-17.00. *Métro:* Porte Dorée.

Arts Décoratifs 107-109 Rue de Rivoli, 1e [7A3]. Panorama of daily life in France from medieval times to early 20th century: furniture, tapestries, ceramics, jewellery, and musical instruments. Open daily except Mon 10.00-12.00 and 14.00-17.00. *Métro:* Pyramides, Palais Royal, Tuileries.

Art Moderne de la Ville, 11 Avenue du President Wilson, 16e [1F3]. Some sculpture but mainly works of neo-Impressionists (Seurat) and abstract painters, with the cubists (Picasso, Braque) given pride of place. Open daily except Mon 10.00-17.30, Wed until 20.30. *Métro:* Iéna.

Arts et Métiers (see Techniques).

Baccarat 30 bis, Rue de Paradis, 10e [4D4]. Sumptuous collection of light-reflecting crystalware from the town of that name in the Vosges. Open daily except Sun 09.00-17.30. Free. *Métro:* Gare de l'Est.

Balzac 47 Rue Raynouard, 16e [5B1]. In the house where he lived, portraits, caricatures, statues, personal objects, and documents relating to the great writer. Open daily 10.00-12.00 and 14.00-18.00 (17.00 winter). *Métro:* Passy, La Muette.

Beaux Arts Petit Palais, Avenue Winston Churchill, 8e[7A2]. Diverse collection built round works of 19th-century French artists, from Ingres to the Impressionists. Open daily except Mon and Tue 10.00-17.00. *Métro:* Champs-Elysées-Clemenceau.

Bourdelle 16 Rue Antoine Bourdelle, 15e [6D6]. Studios, built round small garden, house the hundred and more works of the sculptor: statues, paintings, and sketches. Open daily 10.00-17.50. *Métro:* Falguière; Montparnasse-Bienvenue.

Branly 19 Rue d'Assas, 6e [7C1]. Objects illustrating the birth of radio, with transmitters, receivers, and the first radio message – the historic telegram sent by Marconi in England to Branly in France in 1899. Open daily except Sun 09.00-12.00 and 14.00-18.00. Free. *Métro:* Rennes.

Carnavalet 23 Rue de Sévigné, 3e [8A5]. In fine 16th-century mansion, incomparable collection illustrating history of Paris over the last 400 years: signs and notices, views of monuments, historic scenes and portraits of Parisians, with special emphasis on the Revolution and Empire. Open daily except Mon 10.00-17.50. *Métro:* St Paul.

Cernuschi 7 Avenue Velasquez, 8e [2C5]. Art of China and Japan in various forms, from archaic ceramics and bronzes to contemporary paintings. Open daily except Mon 10.00-17.30. *Métro:* Villiers-Monceau.

Chasse et Nature 60 Rue des Archives, 3e [7A4]. In well restored 18th-century mansion, collection of sporting guns ancient and modern, stuffed animals of many countries and surprising as it may seem, Flemish tapestries and paintings. Open daily except Tue 10.00-18.00 (17.00 winter). *Métro:* Hôtel de Ville, Rambuteau.

Cinéma (Cinémathèque), Palais de Chaillot, (Paris wing), Avenue Albert de Mun, 16e [5F3]. Models, costumes, posters, manuscripts and other items from 70 years of cinema. More a cultural centre than a museum, with frequent exhibitions and film shows. Open daily except Tue 10.00-12.00 and 14.00-17.00. *Métro:* Trocadéro.

Clemenceau 8 Rue Franklin, 16e [5A2]. On view in the house where the Tiger lived for 34 years until his death in 1929, exhibits reveal that the statesman was also a writer and painter. Guided visits. Open Tue, Thur, Sat, and Sun 14.00-17.00 (closed Aug). *Métro:* Trocadéro, Passy.

Cluny 6 Place Paul Painlevé, 5e [7B3]. End-products of arts and crafts of Middle Ages displayed in flamboyant 15th-century town house of abbots of Cluny: furniture, iron-work, pottery, jewellery, sculpture, and tapestries, the last including the celebrated *Dame à la Licorne,* a six-part 15th-century French masterpiece. Open daily except Tue 09.45-12.45 and 14.00-17.15. *Métro:* Odéon, St Michel.

Cognacq-Jay 25 Boulevard des Capucines, 2e [3E1]. Palatial 18th-century home bequeathed to city by founder of the Samaritaine chain of department stores, with walls lined with panelling of the Louis XV period. Pastels by Quentin de la Tour and paintings by Watteau, Fragonard, and others, including Rembrandt's last work. Open daily except Mon 10.00-17.50. *Métro:* Opéra.

Palais de la Découverte Avenue Franklin D. Roosevelt, 8e [2E5]. Vast display illustrating scientific discoveries in lay terms which incorporates a planetarium (afternoons only). Open daily except Mon 10.00-18.00. *Métro:* Franklin D. Roosevelt, Champs-Elysées-Clemenceau.

Delacroix 6 Rue de Furstenberg, 6e [7B2]. Home and studio of the great romantic painter containing modest collection of personal objects along with some of his canvases and sketches. Open daily except Tue 10.00-17.00. *Métro:* Mabillon, St Germain des Près.

Grévin 10 Boulevard Montmartre, 9e [3E3]. The Paris equivalent of Madame Tussaud's, founded in 1882, with waxwork reconstructions of historic scenes and famous people past and present. Open Mon to Fri 14.00-19.00, Sat and Sun 13.00-20.00. *Métro:* Montmartre.

Guimet 6 Place d'Iéna, 16e [5E3]. Incomparable collection of art of the inscrutable Orient: China, Tibet, Japan, Indochina, and central Asia, ranging from buddhas and porcelain to stamps and jewellery. Open daily except Tue 09.45-12.00 and 13.30-17.15. *Métro:* Iéna.

Gustave-Moreau 14 Rue de la Rochefoucauld, 9e [3c2]. In the studio-cum-home designed for him by his architect father, 1,000 paintings and 7,000 sketches by Gustave Moreau (1826-1898), all illustrating his strange world of symbols, visions, and mythologies. Open daily except Tue and Sun 10.00-13.00 and 14.00-17.00. *Métro:* Trinité.

Histoire de France (Archives Nationales), 60 Rue des Francs Bourgeois, 3e [8A5]. In sumptuous 18th-century setting, exhibits illustrating the history of France divided into the Middle Ages, Revolution, and Empire: treaties, papal bulls, MSS, diary of Louis XVI, the only authentic portrait of Joan of Arc, the written abdication of Napoleon and much else. Open daily except Tue 14.00-17.00. *Métro:* Hôtel de Ville, Rambuteau.

Histoire Naturelle Jardin des Plantes, 36 rue Geoffroy St Hilaire 5e [8c5]. Galleries of anatomical specimens, minerals, fossils, mushrooms, and insects. Open daily except Tue 14.00-17.00. *Métro:* Monge, Jussieu.

Homme Palais de Chaillot, (Passy wing), Place du Trocadéro, 16e [1F3]. Fascinating historical study of man showing human types and costumes from all over the world. Includes library, projection room, and restaurant. Open daily except Tue 10.00-17.00 Sat and Sun 10.00-20.00. *Métro:* Trocadéro.

Impressionnisme Jeu de Paume, Tuileries Gardens (Rue de Rivoli), 1e [3E1]. Annexe of Louvre housing on two floors vast collection of paintings by the Impressionists: Manet, Monet, Sisley, Renoir, Pissaro, and others. Open daily except Tue 09.45-17.15. *Métro:* Concorde.

Jacquemart-André 158 Boulevard Haussmann, 8e [2D5]. Superb 19th-century mansion containing rich collection of paintings, sculpture, tapestries, furniture, and works of art of the Italian Renaissance and 18th-century France. Works by Canaletto, Van Dyck, Frans Hals, Rembrandt, and Rubens. Open daily Wed to Sun 13.30-17.00. *Métro:* St Philippe du Roule.

Légion d'Honneur Hôtel de Salm, 2 Rue de Bellechasse, 7e [7A1]. French and foreign decorations, from the age of chivalry to present day, with section devoted to Order of Malta. Open daily except Mon 14.00-17.00. *Métro:* Solférino.

Libération Hôtel des Invalides, Pavillon Robert de Cotte, 51 bis Boulevard Latour-Maubourg, 7e [6B5]. Documents and other exhibits covering the Occupation of France by the Germans, the Resistance and deportation, with letters of General de Gaulle, who created the Ordre de la Libération in 1940. Entirely separate from the nearby Musée de l'Armée. Open daily except Sun 14.00-17.00. *Métro:* Latour-Maubourg.

Louvre Quai du Louvre, 1e [3F2 and 7A2]. Other entrances in Square du Carrousel, Pavillon de Sully, and Pavillon de Flore). Biggest museum in world, with vast collections of all periods and civilizations arranged in rooms and galleries that take four hours to walk round – without stopping. Original collection assembled by François I and enriched by Louis XIV, XV, and XVI, Napoleon (with booty brought back from his campaigns in Italy and elsewhere), and many private donors. Exhibits divided among six departments: Greco-Roman, Oriental and Egyptian antiquities, painting, sculpture, furniture, and jewellery. Most people agree that outstanding sights are the *Venus de Milo* statue, the winged *Victoire de Samothrace,* the *Joconde* (better known to us as the Mona Lisa) and the 137-carat Regent diamond. Guided visits mornings and afternoons; *autoguidage* (portable tape recordings) available in some sections. Photography permitted though fee payable for using a tripod. Cafeteria. Open daily except Tue 09.45-20.00. *Métro:* Louvre.

Marine Palais de Chaillot (Passy wing), Place du Trocadéro 16e [1E3]. Richest maritime collection in world, covering naval and merchant shipping, fishing and pleasure craft, with magnificent paintings by Vernet of French ports and some fine models. Open daily except Tue 10.00-17.00. *Métro:* Trocadéro.

Marmottan 2 Rue Louis Boilly, 16e [5A1]. Two museums in one with furniture, paintings, sculpture, etc, from the 13th to the 19th century, and 100 canvases by Monet (including the famous *Impression: soleil levant* from which the Impressionist school gets its name) along with 50 by Renoir, Sisley, Manet, and others. Open daily except Mon 10.00-18.00. *Métro:* La Muette.

Monnaie Quai de Conti, 6e [7A2]. Medals and coins from ancient Gaul to present day, tours of the State workshops where coins are struck. Open daily except Mon and Wed 14.15-15.30 Sun 11.00-17.00. Free. *Métro:* Pont Neuf; Odéon; St Michel.

Montmartre 11 Rue Poulbot, 18e [3B3]. Waxwork reconstructions of historic moments on the famous *butte* or hill. Guided visits. Open daily 10.00-12.00 and 14.00-18.00. *Métro:* Anvers.

Monuments Français Palais de Chaillot (Paris wing), Place du Trocadéro, 16e [1F3]. Based on an idea of Viollet-le-Duc, prodigious restorer of medieval buildings, architectural and monumental works from Gallo-Roman period to 19th century: portals, tombs, calvaries, fountains, and frescoes. Open daily except Tue 09.45-12.30 and 14.00-17.15. *Métro:* Trocadéro.

Conservatoire de Musique 11 Rue de Madrid, 8e [2C6]. Some 2,000 musical instruments dating from the 16th to the 20th century, including several Stradivarius, Marie Antoinette's harp, and Beethoven's clavichord. Open Wed and Sat 14.00-16.30. *Métro:* Europe.

Opéra 1 Place Charles Garnier, 9e [3E2]. Busts, portraits, photographs and personal possessions of famous artists, plus library of 80,000 volumes covering music and dance. Open daily except Sun 10.00-17.00. *Métro:* Opéra.

Plans-Reliefs Hôtel des Invalides, Corridor de Metz, 7e [6A5]. Astonishing collection of model towns, forts and other structures created during the reign of Louis XIV by Louvois and enriched by Louis XV, Napoleon I, Louis Philippe, and Napoleon III. Open daily except Sun morning and Tue 10.00-18.00 (17.00 winter). *Métro:* Invalides, Latour-Maubourg, Varenne.

Préfecture de Police 36 Quai des Orfèvres, 1e [7B3]. Summonses and other documents relating to criminals and prisoners, gruesome objects used in famous crimes, and exhibits illustrating the development of the PJ or Police Judiciaire in the capital. Free. Open Thu 14.00-17.00. *Métro:* Cité, St Michel.

Postal 34 Boulevard de Vaugirard, 15e [6D6]. Everything of interest to philatelists, from stamps to the evolution of postal services by land, sea, and air. Open daily except Thu 10.00-17.00. *Métro:* Montparnasse-Bienvenue.

Rodin Hotel Biron, 77 Rue de Varenne, 7e [6A6]. Works of the famous sculptor Auguste Rodin (1840-1917), including the celebrated Kiss, and series devoted to Balzac, the female form, and human hands. Open daily except Tue 10.00-12.45 and 14.00-17.00. *Métro:* Varenne.

Santé Militaire (Val de Grace), 277 bis Rue St Jacques, 5e [7D3]. On first floor of cloister, specialized collection relating to military medicine: treatment of wounded, transport designed for them, models of ambulances and hospitals, and much else. Open daily except Sat and Sun 09.00-11.00 and 13.00-17.00. *Métro:* Port Royal.

Techniques Conservatoire des Arts et Métiers, 292 Rue St Martin, 3e [4E4]. Illustrations, models and examples of technical conquests through the ages, including 17th-century clocks and an electric cigar lighter of 1892, housed partly in the ancient priory of St Martin des Champs. Open daily 12.00-17.45. *Métro:* Réaumur-Sébastopol.

Victor Hugo Hôtel d'Arnaud, 6 Place des Vosges, 4e [8A6]. In the house where he lived from 1832 to 1838, documents and personal possessions of the writer, some of them illustrating his obsession with fantasy and death. Open daily except Mon 10.00-17.50. *Métro:* Chemin Vert, St Paul, Bastille.

Vieux Montmartre 17 Rue St Vincent, 18e [3B3]. Beneath the famous vineyard, modest evocation of the history of the old village and its people, from the merely eccentric to the talented. Open daily except Tue 14.30-17.30. *Métro:* Lamarck-Caulaincourt.

13. Where to stay

Paris has the reputation of being the most expensive city in Europe but in fact it is still possible to live more cheaply there than in many other places. There are some 500 simple, clean, and well run hotels in the capital, the widest choice being around the Gare du Nord, on the Left Bank and, believe it or not, in Montmartre. But there are fewer to choose from in August when, being family-run, many small hotels close.

Generally, prices get lower the farther out you go, though the saving on hotel bills is offset by the cost of travelling. Few of the cheaper hotels have a restaurant, which is just as well since it leaves you free to eat wherever you happen to be.

In Paris, as elsewhere in France, two can often sleep as cheaply as one, since hotels charge not per person but by the room. Some hotels even have rooms for four people, ideal for friends of the same sex or parents with young children. The city is always full of people and, since the lower-priced hotels are in greatest demand, some people argue that it is sensible to book ahead. It is, if you have stayed at the hotel before. But not all hotels are reliable and no one should take a room until he has seen it and checked the price. French hoteliers expect this and are not in the least embarrassed when asked if they have something cheaper.

Along with the basic items of furniture, rooms in modest hotels are likely to be equipped only with a *cabinet de toilette* (handbasin with hot and cold water and possibly a *bidet*), with the wc or *water* down the hall. Breakfast (usually served in the room) is almost always an extra and seemingly expensive for what you get (coffee or tea, rolls, butter and jam).

In the following list of hotels A denotes those with double rooms at under 50 francs, B those from 50 to 100 francs.

Bastille

Place Voltaire (B), 132 Boulevard Voltaire, 11e [8F6]. (Tel 700.39.83). 42 rooms, no restaurant

Etoile

Boursault (A), 15 Rue Boursault, 17e [2c6]. (Tel. 522.42.19). 13 rooms, no restaurant

Gare du Nord

Chabrol (A), 46 Rue de Chabrol, 10e [4D4]. (Tel 770.10.77). 28 rooms, no restaurant

Europe (B), 98 Boulevard Magenta, 10e [4c4]. (Tel 607.25.82). 38 rooms, no restaurant

Grands Boulevards

Lafayette Buffault (B), 6 Rue Buffault, 9e [3D3]. (Tel 770.70.96). 48 rooms, no restaurant

Laval (A), 11 Rue Victor Massé, 9e [3c2]. (Tel 878.73.49). 26 rooms, no restaurant

Montpensier (B), 12 Rue de Richelieu, 1e [3F2]. (Tel 296.28.50). 24 rooms, no restaurant

Invalides

Résidence du Champ de Mars (A), 19 Rue du Champ de Mars, 7e [6A5]. (Tel 705.25.45). 36 rooms, no restaurant

Rosaria (A), 42 Boulevard Garibaldi, 15e [6c4]. (Tel 783.20.10). 35 rooms, no restaurant

Left Bank

Arts (A), 8 Rue Coypel, 13e [8F4]. (Tel 331.22.30). 46 rooms, no restaurant

Grandes Ecoles (B), 75 Rue du Cardinal Lemoine, 5e [8c4]. (Tel 326.79.23). 44 rooms

Pacific (A), 8 Rue Philippe de Champaigne, 13e [8F4]. (Tel 331.17.06). 50 rooms, no restuarant

Luxembourg

Floridor (A), 28 Place Denfert-Rochereau, 14e [7F2]. (Tel 326.90.73). 45 rooms

Marronniers (B), 21 Rue Jacob, 6e [8E6]. (Tel 033.91.66). 22 rooms

Marais

Résidence Magenta (B), 35 Rue Y. Toudic, 10e [4E5]. (Tel 607.63.13). 29 rooms, no restaurant

Montmartre

Puy de Dôme (B), 18 Rue Ordener, 18e [4A5].
(Tel 627.78.55). 27 rooms, no restaurant, closed Aug

Residence Becquerel (A), 6 Rue Becquerel, 18e [3A3].
(Tel 076.79.20). 24 rooms

Montparnasse

Bréa (A), 14 Rue Bréa, 6e [7D1]. (Tel 033.76.21). 27 rooms,
no restaurant

Parc (A), 60 Rue Beaunier, 14e [7F2]. (Tel 540.77.02). 29·
rooms, no restaurant

Right Bank

Ducs de Bourgogne (B), 19 Rue du Pont Neuf, 1e [7A3].
(Tel 233.95.64). 44 rooms, no restaurant

Europe (B), 15 Rue Constantinople, 8e [2C6].
(Tel 522.80.80). 50 rooms, no restaurant, closed Aug

Ministère (B), 31 Rue du Surène, 8e [2E6]. (Tel 266.21.43).
36 rooms, no restaurant

Auberges de Jeunesse (Youth Hostels)

The following list is only a selection of those in the central
area; there are many more, particularly on the southern
outskirts of the city.

Centre International 20 Rue Jean Jacques Rousseau, 1e
[1F3]. (Tel 236.88.18). Seasonal. Mixed, 18-30.

Centre Maxime-Ducarme, 14 Rue du General Humbert, 14e
[7F3]. (Tel 250.55.63). All year. Mixed.

Le Fauconnier, 11 Rue du Fauconnier, 4e [8B5].
(Tel 272.99.12). All year. Mixed, 15-30.

Foyer des Francs-Bourgeois, 21 Rue St Antoine, 4e [8B6].
(Tel 272.19.00). Seasonal. Mixed, 18-30.

Foyer des Services de Jeunesse Féminine, 70 Avenue
Denfert-Rochereau, 14e [7E2]. (Tel 326.92.84). Seasonal.
Girls, 16-25.

Foyer International d'Accueil de Paris, 30 Rue Cabanis, 14e
[7F2]. (Tel 707.25.69). All year. Mixed, 18-30.

Foyer Notre Dame, 5 Rue Lagrange, 5e [7B3]. (Tel 033.49.96). Seasonal. Girls, 15-30.

Foyer St Michel, 103 Rue de Lille, 7e [7A1]. (Tel 551.11.39). Seasonal. Girls, 18-30.

Maison des Etudiants, 214 Boulevard Raspail, 14e [7B1]. (Tel 633.61.30). Seasonal. Mixed students, 18-30.

Maison Jeanne d'Arc, 21 Rue du General Bertrand, 7e [6C5]. (Tel 734.75.17). Seasonal. Students, 18-30.

La Nef, 10 Rue de Richelieu, 1e [3F2]. (Tel 742.30.90). All year. Girls, 18-30.

Relais d'Accueil, 21 Rue des Malmaisons, 13e [4F4]. (Tel 588.12.61). All year. Mixed, 18-30.

Residence Internationale Carrefour, 63 Rue Monsieur le Prince, 5e [7B2]. (Tel 326.87.66). Seasonal. Students, 20-30.

Camping

Well equipped campsites exist on the eastern and western outskirts of Paris. Both accept tent campers, motor-caravanners and trailer caravanners alike.

Bois de Boulogne: Camp TCF****, Route du Bord de L'Eau. Entry no later than 12.00 in summer. Minibus service to nearest métro (Port de Neuilly).

Champigny: Camp TCF****, Quai de Polangis, Champigny. 15km E, via Porte de Charenton and A4/N4. Beside the river Marne.

14. Where to eat

Compared with London, restaurant meals in Paris are much more varied and usually better value. The French set more store by good food than most of us do and are willing to pay more for it. But they are also prepared to criticize the food they are served; more than anything else, this helps to keep up standards.

Paris dominates France as few other capitals do, in cooking as in everything else. Family-run restaurants specializing in the dishes native to one or other ancient province exist in many parts of the city. On the Left Bank particularly, they often adjoin equally modest places just as dedicated to the food of countries which once formed part of France's colonial empire. Typical examples are the Moroccan, Algerian, and Tunisian restaurants around St Séverin, where native dishes like *couscous* (a subtly-spiced stew of meat or fish and vegetables served on a bed of roughly ground and steamed semolina wheat with a hot sauce) are washed down with drinkable but inexpensive wines from the same countries, one with the unlikely name of Mascara. French cuisine is world-famous and has developed a language all its own: *Sole Dieppoise,* for example, means sole as it would normally be prepared in Dieppe, with a variety of other seafood. Many other dishes bear the names of those who invented them or the historical figures to whom they were dedicated: the composer himself created *Tournedos Rossini* or fillet steak cooked with goose liver pâté on top, but *Pêche Melba* was invented by the famous chef Escoffier for the equally well known opera singer. Some menu terms can be downright misleading: *Assiette anglaise* is a collation of cold meats, some of them raw; and *crudités* are grated raw vegetables served as hors d'oeuvres.

Many main dishes come ungarnished, the vegetables being served as a separate course. But some terms on the menu refer not so much to the way the dish is cooked as to the kind of vegetables served with it. Two examples are *Nicoise*, which usually means with courgettes, black olives, and garlic, and *Bourguignonne,* with button mushrooms, onions, and bacon. Anyone squeamish over food should learn by heart the French for frogs' legs *(cuisses de grenouilles)* and snails *(escargots)*.

Soups are invariably good and are usually served at dinner rather than at lunchtime. Bread is put on the table as a matter of course and within reason you can eat as much as you like. But butter (except perhaps with cheese) is usually an extra. The French prefer their meat underdone but if you like yours cooked you should order it *bien cuit.* Though it will still probably turn up more raw than you would like. Usually, cheese is an alternative to a sweet, though on some menus the two are included. In which case the cheese will come before and not after the dessert.

Restaurants

The only way to eat on a budget in Paris is to stick to fixed-price menus, checking beforehand that they are *service compris.* Better still, unless you are really hungry, patronize those places offering a *plat du jour* or single main dish. But be warned that both are often served only at accepted mealtimes, say 12.00 to 13.00 and 18.30 to 20.30, and that even when they are displayed outside you may have to persist in asking for them. The menu usually includes three courses, service and taxes, and sometimes the house wine.

On Sundays, when most modest restaurants close and others double their prices, buy wine, bread and pâté from one of the food shops that stay open until noon and have a picnic in the park.

Usually, one kind of restaurant to avoid is the self-service. The staff change almost weekly and are often indifferent to the food they serve and the people who foolishly eat it. Avoid snack bars, too. For the price of a sandwich at one of them you can probably buy a proper meal. And splashing out on a *grand café au lait* several times a day will soon make a hole in your pocket. Instead, go to a stand-up bar for a *café simple.*

Anyone who wants to visit Paris and survive might do worse than try the following short list of restaurants, some of the cheapest in the capital. With a little effort, any visitor can find many others like them. (The letter A denotes a meal for under 25 francs, B one for from 25 to 45 francs).

Ancien Chartier (A), 7 Rue du Faubourg Montmartre, 9e [3E3] open 12.00-13.30 and 18.00-21.30

Athenian (A), 26 Rue François, 8e [2E4]

Auberge de Jarente (B), 7 Rue de Jarente, 4e [8B5]

Bonne Table (A), 5 Rue Séveste, 18e [3B3]

Brouillet (A), 5 Rue Paul Lelong, 2e [3E3]

Butte aux Moulins (A), 74 Rue des Martyrs, 18e [3C2]

Charpentiers (B), 10 Rue Mabillon, 6e [7B2]. Closed Sat, Sun, and August

Chez Paul (B), 15 Place Dauphine, 6e [7A3]. Closed August

Epi d'Or (A), 25 Rue Jean Jacques Rousseau, 1e [3F3]. Closed August

Grand Colbert (A), 2 bis Rue Vivienne, 2e [3F2]

Gourmet de l'Ile (B), 42 Rue St Louis en l'Ile, 4e [8B4]. Closed Thu and August

l'Incroyable (A), 26 Rue de Richelieu, 1e [3F2]. Closed Sun

Jardin de la Mouffe (B), 75 Rue Mouffetard, 5e [8D4]

Julien (A), 16 Rue du Faubourg St Denis, 10e [4E4]. Closed Sun and August

Julien et Petit (B), 40 Rue de l'Université, 7e [7A1]

Léna et Mimile (A), 2 Place Lucien Herr, 5e [7D3]

Menestrel (A), 53 Rue St Louis en l'Ile, 4e [7B4]

Perraudin (A), 157 Rue St Jacques, 5e [7D3]

Petite Chaise (B), 36 Rue de Grenelle, 7e [5D1]

Petit St Benoit (B), 4 Rue St Benoit, 6e [7A2]. Closed Sat Sun, and mid-July to mid-August

Rendezvous des Camionneurs (A), 72 Quai des Orfèvres, 1e [7A3]

Rougeot (A), 59 Boulevard du Montparnasse, 6e [7D1]. Closed July

Saints Pères (B), 175 Boulevard St Germaine, 6e [7B1]

Vagenende (A), 142 Boulevard St Germain, 6e [7B2]

Prices at English-style *tavernes* like the Bedford Arms near the Odéon are high. More rewarding in their tariffs and atmosphere are the bars patronized by students and local people. An added bonus is that most such places serve the wines of a particular region (like Burgundy or the Loire) along with a wide choice of tasty food: pâté, ham on the bone, garlic sausage, mussels, and the like. The following short list is only a sample:

L'Académie du Vin, Passage Berryer (off Rue Royale), 8e [2E6]. Welcoming bistrot run by an Englishman, an authority on French wines

Café Belge, 88 bis Boulevard du Port Royal, 5e [7E3]. Fascinating range of beers from all over Europe

La Cloche des Halles, 28 Rue Coquillière, 1e [3F3]

Ma Bourgogne, 19 Place des Vosges, 4e [8B5]

Rocher de Tombelaine, 5 Rue de la Cossonnerie, 1e [4F4]

Le Sancerre, 22 Avenue Rapp, 7e [2F4]

Au Sauvignon, 80 Rue des Saints Pères, 6e [7B1]

15. Parks, Gardens and Excursions

Tuesdays, when most museums and other public buildings are closed, is the day to go the the parks, where there is a lot to see and do. The two biggest, the 'lungs' of Paris, are the great woods of Boulogne and Vincennes, the first on the west, the second on the east.

The Buttes Chaumont

An undulating and picturesque small park east of the Gare de l'Est, the Buttes Chaumont is centred on a lake enclosing an island from which there are unusual views of the Sacré Coeur. It contains puppet theatres, children's play areas, and several good restaurants. It stays open until midnight in summer. (métro: Buttes Chaumont.)

The Bois de Boulogne

The Bois de Boulogne takes its name from a long-vanished church dedicated in the 14th century to Notre Dame de Boulogne, patron saint of the fishing port on the Channel coast. The forest was enclosed by Henri II in 1556, and a century later Colbert converted it into a royal hunting ground, with straight 'rides' marked at their junctions by crosses. Thrown open to the public by Louis XIV, it did not become fashionable until the Regency. The Longchamp racecourse is on the western edge, Auteuil on the eastern. The high speed ring road *(boulevards périphériques)* tunnels under the eastern edge. Adjoining Auteuil are the Lac Supérieur and, to the north of it, the larger Lac Inférieur. West of the Lac Inférieur is the Pré Catalan, a well tended area incorporating the Shakespeare Garden, planted with trees, herbs and flowers mentioned in the plays.

Near the Seine in the northwest corner of the park is the Bagatelle, a château built in three months in the 18th century by the Count of Artois, later Charles X. In the 19th century it was owned by the Hertford family, who sold it to the City of Paris in 1906. The building is less famous than the garden surrounding it. Along the northern edge of the Bois de Boulogne is the Jardin d'Acclimation or children's amusement park, open from 09.00 to 19.00 in summer, until dusk in winter. It includes a small zoo, a miniature railway and car track, puppet and open air theatres, amusement arcade, and boating lake. (métro: Porte Maillot, Porte Dauphine, Porte d'Auteuil, Sablons).

The Bois de Vincennes

The Bois de Boulogne tends to empty at weekends, just the time when the Bois de Vincennes usually fills up. Dominated by its château, at the northern edge, and dotted with lakes, the park takes at least a day to explore fully. Completed by Charles V in 1370, the original château was used as a prison from the early 16th century until the Revolution, when the prisoners included Fouquet, who incurred the wrath of Louis XIV by building the château of Vaux-le-Vicomte, more impressive than anything the king then possessed. The classical part of the building, consisting of two symmetrical pavilions framing the main courtyard, were designed by Le Vau in 1654. Under Napoleon the château was turned into an arsenal, the towers being cut level with the perimeter wall and the keep once more used as a prison. In August 1944 the retreating Germans mined the building, damaging the ramparts and the pavilions. Subsequently restored, it now looks much as it did in the 17th century.

A popular feature of the park is the Floral Garden, open daily from 09.30 to 18.30, created for the 1969 flower show and containing a lake, flower and water gardens, and other attractions.

But the most famous feature is the zoo or Parc Zoologique, with the animals and birds kept mostly in open-air enclosures. There is a superb aquarium, too, in the Parc Floral (open 09.30 to 18.30), which covers 70 acres. (métro: Porte Dorée.)

Père-Lachaise

Biggest and most important of the Paris cemeteries is Père-Lachaise, which takes its name from the Jesuit priest and confessor to Louis IX, whose home was nearby. An astonishing place, where lovers meet and mothers walk their children. Among the famous names on the tombs are Rossini, Chopin, Bizet, Sarah Bernhardt, Oscar Wilde, Colette, and Edith Piaf. (métro: Père Lachaise.)

Boat trips on the Seine

One of the best ways to see Paris is from the river, from which many of the finest buildings are visible. River launches leave from four different points. All charge less in the mornings and most give reductions for children. As a rule, a commentary is given in several languages, including English. Departure points are: *Pont de l'Alma* (métro: Alma Marceau) daily every 30 minutes from 10.00 to 12.00 and 14.00 to 18.30, *Pont d'Iéna* (métro: Iéna) every 30 minutes from 09.30 to 19.00 in season and 10.00 to 17.30 the rest of the year. *Quai de Montébello* (métro: St Michel) every 30 minutes from 10.00 to 12.00 and 14.00 to 18.30, and *Square du Vert Galant* (métro: Cité) at 10.30, 11.15 and 12.00 then every 30 minutes from 13.30 to 18.00. The meals served on some services are very expensive.

The Catacombes

The entrance to the Catacombes is in one of the pavilions at the junction of the Avenue de Général Leclerc and the Place Denfert Rochereau [7E2]. Housing the bones of six million Parisians, including the skeletons transferred from the Cimetière des Innocents near Les Halles in 1786, the ossuary is open at 14.00 on Saturdays.

The Sewers

Tours of the sewers built in the 19th century by Haussmann take place on various afternoons from July to September. Dates and times can be obtained by telephoning 331.70.00. The assembly point is at the junction of the Pont de l'Alma and the Quai d'Orsay [2F4].

Basilica of St Denis

Famed for its vast vestibule, its painted and gilded interior and its carved choir stalls, the majestic 12th-century basilica dedicated to St Denis, patron saint and protector of France, is in the northern suburbs beyond the Porte de la Chapelle. A landmark in French history, it is the burial place of most of the French kings and their families. In the immense transept are the splendid mausoleums of Louis XII, François I, and Henri II as well as scores of medieval effigies and funeral statues. Conducted tours of the church take place daily from April to September every 30 minutes from 10.00 to 11.30 and 14.00 to 17.00.

Versailles

Once he had seen the château of his minister of finance (Vaux-le-Vicomte near Melun, to the southeast) Louis XIV's conceit drove him to build Versailles, using the same trinity of artists: landscaping by Le Nôtre, architectural design by Le Vau, and interior decoration by Le Brun. Looted at the Revolution, the palace is a mere shell compared with the original, when it housed a court of 6,000 people. But enough is left to gain an impression of what this intimidating structure was like in its heyday and to understand why, in the face of such luxury, the French Revolution took place. Versailles is 14 miles west of Paris and is easily reached by motorway.

Fontainebleau

Forty miles southeast of Paris, Fontainebleau is much older than Versailles, for parts of it date from the 12th century. Called the 'exhibition of French architecture from the 12th to the 19th century', its main sights are the beautiful renaissance ballroom and the voracious carp in the lake. The château is famous for its associations with Napoleon I. Trains leave the Gare de Lyon for Fontainebleau, reached by car on the A6 motorway.

16. Shopping

The pride of Paris is its shops, from humble boutiques to the department stores covering several blocks. Along the Rue de Rivoli the shopping is more popular on the east (Bazar de l'Hôtel de Ville, Samaritaine), more bourgeois on the west (Louvre). Of the department stores, Au Printemps and Galeries Lafayette, off the Boulevard Haussmann near the Opéra, are among the most elegant, the Prisunic and Monoprix chains cheaper. On the Left Bank, at Sèvres-Babylone, Bon Marché remains somewhat isolated.

Department stores and the other big shops stay open 09.30 to 18.30 every day except Tuesday and Sunday. Smaller family-run shops tend to stay open later, but close from 12.00 to 14.00.

Despite present-day uniformity Paris has kept its quarters specializing in different products, furniture around the Bastille, perfumes at the Opéra, jewellery around the Place Vendôme, clothes at the Rond Point and along the Champs Elysées, cars at the Etoile, and antiques along the Quai Voltaire. Parisians go to the Châtelet for pet birds, to the Boulevard St Michel for books, and to the Rue de Seine for paintings.

The best-known shopping street is the pedestrians-only Rue Mouffetard [8D4], continued on the north by the Place de la Contrescarpe. There are a dozen or so streets where articles are cheaper than elsewhere: they include the Faubourg St Denis [4E4], the Rue du Montorgueil [3F3] near Les Halles, the Avenue de St Ouen and Rue Lepic [3B2] in Montmartre.

Biggest of the markets is the Marché aux Puces (Flea Market) at the Porte de Clignancourt, near the express ring road on the north. Here, as at other places, the best plan is to buy around midday rather than first thing, for prices drop as the day wears on. Other, smaller markets are the Ménilmontant (Boulevard de Belleville, 11e, Tue and Wed); St Quentin (Boulevard Magenta 10e, daily except Mon); Breteuil (Avenue de Saxe, 7e, Thu and Sat), Richard Lenoir (Boulevard Richard Lenoir, 11e, Thu and Sun), St

Germain (Rue Clément, 6e, daily except Mon) and Port Royal (Boulevard du Port Royal, 5e, Tue, Thu and Sat).

North of Montmartre cemetery, the Marché aux Puces at Porte St Ouen takes place on Saturday, Sunday and Monday from 08.00-10.00 to 18.00 (métro: Porte de Clignancourt or Porte St Ouen). The best time to go is around 09.00 on Saturday. The Marché St Pierre [3B/C3], another flea market, is held on Wednesday and Saturday in the Rue de Steinkerque, Place St Pierre, Square Willette and part of Boulevard Rochechouart (métro: Barbès-Rochechouart).

Articles seized by the Customs are sold off cheaply at the Saises de Douane in the Rue des Francs Bourgeois [8A5], in the Marais, and those pawned and not reclaimed suffer a similar fate at the Vente du Monte de Piété, farther along the street.

17. Paris by night

Paris continues to live up to its reputation as the capital of sophisticated pleasures, with every possible kind of night life from bars and discothèques, erotica live and on film, superbly staged revues and cabarets, and a high standard of theatrical drama.

Revues and Cabarets

Many cabarets are expensive and there can be unpleasant surprises in store for anyone who does not check beforehand how much he will have to pay. Places like the Folies Bergère and the Bal du Moulin Rouge are landmarks in the history of Paris, founded as they were during the gay days of the Belle Epoque at the turn of the century. With their fixed-price dinners they are also the safest bet for a night out. The Moulin Rouge in the Place Blanche, on the southern edge of Montmartre, opens nightly at 20.00, serves dinner, and gives diners time to dance before putting on its big revue at 22.00. The equally famous Folies Bergère in the Rue Richer, also at the edge of Montmartre, stages two shows every night except Monday and gives reductions to students. The Lido in the Champs Elysées famed for its beplumed Bluebell girl dancers, serves dinner at 20.30 and puts on two spectacles, as they are called, at 22.30 and 00.45. At all three it is essential to book in advance. These are establishments with a reputation to keep up, but for every one that is good there are ten that are mediocre.

Discotheques

Nowadays *boîte de nuit* means not night club but discothèque. The price of entry is often included in the cost of the obligatory and seemingly costly first drink, though subsequent drinks are usually cheaper. Bearing this in mind, charges are modest to reasonable. Some places allow girls in free of charge. The following is a list of the more popular.

Caveau de la Montagne, 18 Rue Descartes, 5e [7c3]. Well liked by students of the Left Bank.

Poney Club, 25 bis Boulevard Poissonière, 2e [3E3]. Standard pop on two floors, with bar, open Wed and Sun from 21.30 to 03.00.

La Casita, 167 Rue Montmartre, 2e [3E3]. Rhythm and blues, nightly from Wed to Sun 21.30 to 05.00.

La Bohème, 2 Place du Tertre, 18e [3B3]. Live orchestra, nightly from 21.30 to 02.00.

Slow Club, 130 Rue de Rivoli, le [7A3]. High temple of traditional jazz, nightly except Mon from 21.30 to 02.00.

Riverside, 7 Rue Gregoire de Tours 6e [7B2]. One of the most pleasant pop discos in and a spacious floor, open nightly from 21.00 to dawn.

American Style Bars

Gain an insight into the way many Parisians spend their evenings by joining them for a while in one of the American-style bars where soft drinks are just as popular as the other kind and most of the customers, more interested in talking than imbibing, make one drink last several hours.

Harry's Bar in the Rue Daunou, run by a Scot named Andy against a backdrop of 50 different brands of whisky, attracts mostly Americans though French rugby players and fans are among the regulars. Like most others in Paris, the bar stays open until 04.00. The recently restyled bar of the plush hotel George V in the Avenue George V is usually so crowded that the customers spill out into the Grand Salon. Facing the British Embassy in the Rue du Faubourg St Honoré is the Bristol, with the most distinguished bar in Paris, worthy of the last 'grand palace' in France.

One of the most popular bars in St Germain des Près is the Village in the Rue Gozlin, the haunt mostly of writers and comedians, but the Sabot de Bernard in the Rue du Sabot is acknowledged the most elegant. Montparnasse still holds its own with the international set, seen most evenings in the Rosebud in the Rue Delambre.

Most fashionable bar in Paris is the panoramic Concorde Lafayette at Porte Maillot. On the 34th floor, it has a huge window giving a view that stretches from the Défense on one side to Notre Dame on the other.

Theatres and Cinemas

Given time, every visitor to Paris should go at least once to the theatre. Even if he does not speak French he can still get a lot of enjoyment out of the opera, ballet, a musical show, or even the music hall. Sold at most bookstalls, the weekly *Pariscope* gives all the current programmes.

The best seats are the *fauteuils d'orchestre* (stalls), *fauteuils de balcon* (dress circle) and *places de loge* (seats in a box, sometimes sold separately). The *galerie* (upper circle) and *amphitheatre* (gallery) are the cheapest. The best place to buy tickets is at the theatre itself: fees charged by booking agents are often exorbitant. In France, theatres open on Sundays and close one weekday instead. Standards are high but so are prices – 28 to 51 francs a seat at the Theatre Francais, for example.

Grand opera is put on at the Opéra (Place de l'Opéra [3E1]) and plays including masterpieces by French dramatists at the Théâtre Francais (Place du Théâtre Français) and at the Odéon [7c2].

English language films with French subtitles are shown at many cinemas, mostly in the Champs Elysées and the Grands Boulevards (Capucines, Italiens). In both theatres and cinemas, where smoking is forbidden, it is usual to tip the usherette who shows you to your seat.

18. Useful addresses

The Paris Welcome Office (Bureau d'Accueil [2D4]) at 127 Avenue des Champs Elysées (720.04.96) is open from 09.00 to 22.00. The staff give information, literature, and advice on the capital, and will also make hotel bookings.

There are other offices at the Gare du Nord (open 06.30-21.30), Gare de l'Est (open 06.30-13.30 and 16.30-23.30), the Gare de Lyon (open 06.30-10.30 and 17.30-23.30), the Aérogare des Invalides (open 09.00-24.00 Mon to Sat, 10.30-13.30 and 15.30-19.30 Sun), and Montmartre (open 10.00-17.00 Mon to Sat, 10.00-16.00 Sun).

There are *bureaux de change* at most of these as well as at main railway stations like the Gare du Nord. All give more favourable rates of exchange than hotels. Post Offices in each district are open from 08.00 to 19.00. The main post office in Paris is at 52 Rue du Louvre, 1e open day and night all the year round. Lost property can be claimed at the Bureau des Objects Trouvés, 36 Rue des Morillons, 15e [6F4] (Tel 828.97.30), open Mon to Fri 08.30 to 17.00 (métro: Convention).

British Consulate, 37 Rue du Faubourg St Honoré [2E6].

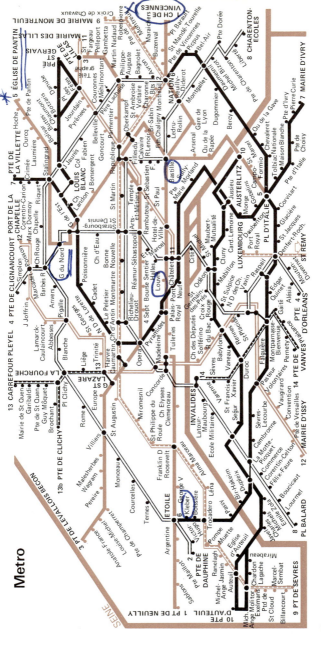

Metro

Map of the city

Key to the map pages

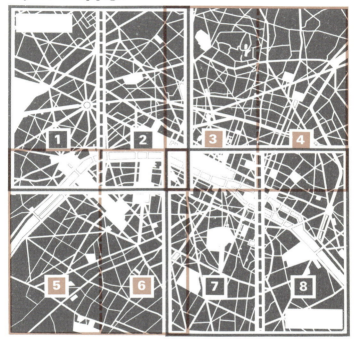

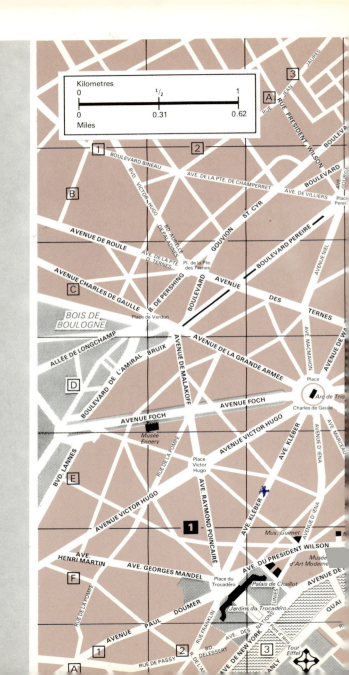

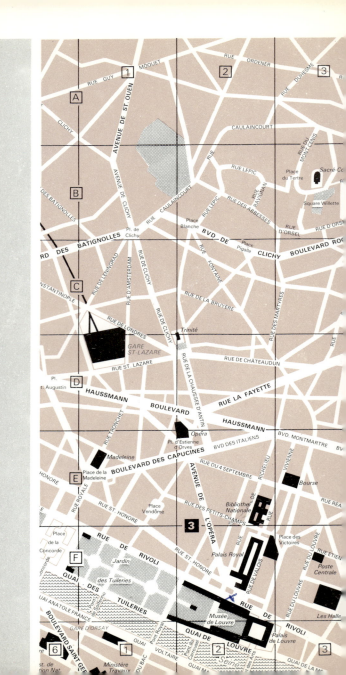

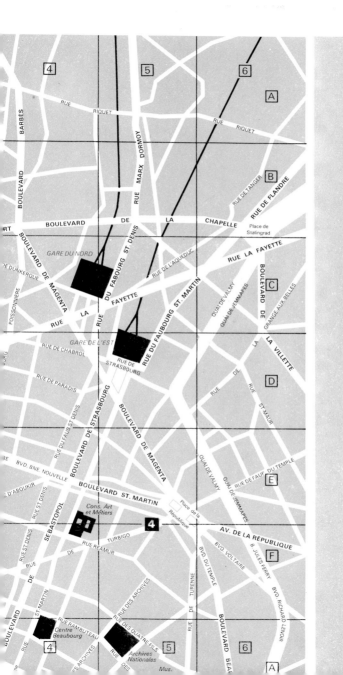

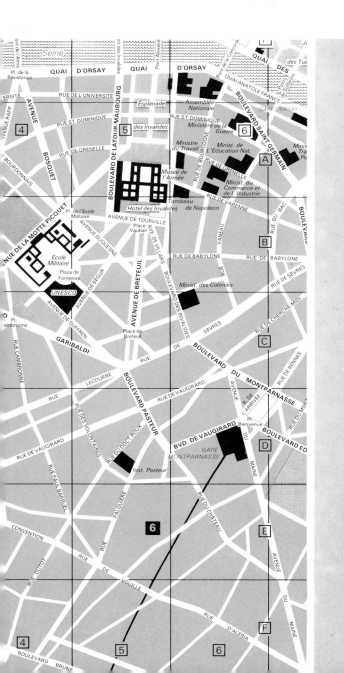

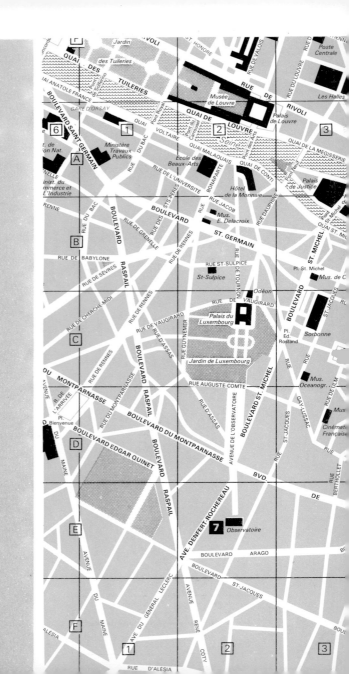

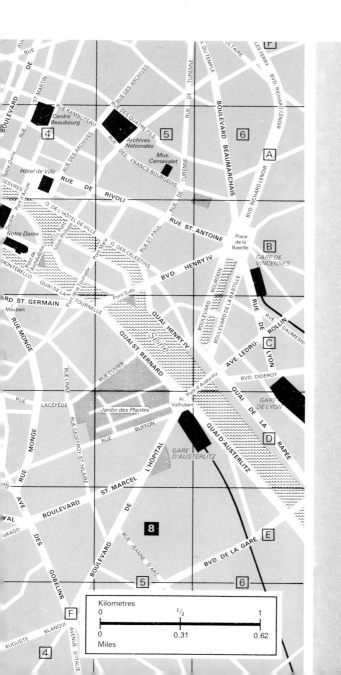

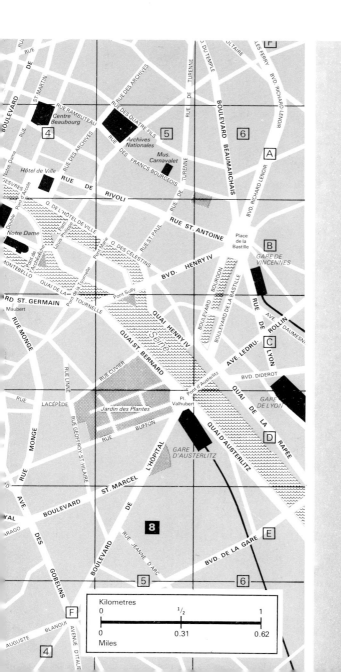

TM30 C09